PLANTS & GARDENS

BROOKLYN BOTANIC GARDEN RECORD

Herbs & Cooking

1990

Brooklyn Botanic Garden

Staff for this issue

ANN LOVEJOY, *Guest Editor*

BARBARA B. PESCH, *Editor*

CHARLES GABELER, *Art Director*

JO KEIM, *Associate Editor*

JANET MARINELLI, *Associate Editor*

and the Editorial Committee of the Brooklyn Botanic Garden

DONALD E. MOORE, *President, Brooklyn Botanic Garden*

ELIZABETH SCHOLTZ, *Director Emeritus*

STEPHEN K-M. TIM, *Vice President, Science & Publications*

Herbs & Cooking

Vol. 45   Handbook #122   Winter 1990   No. 4

CONTENTS

Cover Photograph by   Elvin McDonald

Plants and Gardens, Brooklyn Botanic Garden Record (ISSN 0362-5850) is published quarterly at 1000 Washington Ave., Brooklyn, N.Y. 11225, by the **Brooklyn Botanic Garden, Inc.** Second-class-postage paid at Brooklyn, N.Y. and at additional mailing offices. Subscriptions included in Botanic Garden membership dues ($25.00 per year), which includes newsletters and announcements. Copyright © 1990, 1993 by the Brooklyn Botanic Garden, Inc.
POSTMASTER: Send address changes to BROOKLYN BOTANIC GARDEN, Brooklyn, N.Y. 11225

foreword

Ann Lovejoy

Food is a lot more interesting than it used to be. To the cooks of my New England youth, garlic was a novelty, and onions were treated with suspicion. Herbs were certainly used, if nearly always dried rather than fresh, but hot, spicy foods were virtually unknown. I can remember my parents holding little dinners at which the tables were draped with checkered cloths and decorated with candles in chianti bottles. Very mild chili or spaghetti might be served, accompanied by a raw, garlicky salad of mixed greens. All this seems extremely tame now, but was considered avant-garde at the time.

For many years, the quintessential American meal was Thanksgiving dinner; roast turkey with mashed potatoes and gravy. There might have been a side dish of fancy green beans (drenched with canned mushroom soup and covered with blanched almonds), but easily the snappiest thing on the plate was the cranberry sauce. Now that turkey might well be smoked over applewood or alder, stuffed with oranges or jalapeño cornbread, sauced with an oil-free pesto of walnuts and cilantro. The side dishes might include anything from fresh chutney or plum sauce to homemade orange-tarragon mustard.

Americans are taking new pleasure in their mixed culinary heritage, choosing to pursue multifarious new directions in our astonishingly high-tech kitchens. We have more and fancier cooking gadgets than ever; anybody who wants one boasts an espresso machine, a special steamer for couscous, a ravioli press. Our supermarkets are fuller than ever, and we can buy foods from all over the world nearly any day of the year. Chilean peaches and strawberries fill the markets in January, along with feijoa and star fruits. In the cities, one can find Wensleydale or pecorino cheeses, Tunisian flatbread or blue corn tortillas, Thai fish paste or Chinese kumquats, fresh duck or trout any time. We dine out often and adventurously, having learned to value and appreciate flavors that would have given our grandparents heart attacks—unless our grandparents were not from these shores. For what has happened is that our many culinary traditions are merging; American food is coming of age. Our melting pot society is beginning to produce a new kind of food, an international cuisine that is solidly American in feeling and approach.

Ann Lovejoy is a contributing editor of Horticulture *magazine, writes a garden column for* Seattle Weekly *and is the author of several books on gardening and cooking.*

Fresh foods in prime condition, uncomplicated preparations and savory combinations that emphasize the essential qualities of each ingredient are hallmarks of a new American cuisine. Featured here is a cold carrot soup garnished with fresh chives and thyme.

Fresh foods in prime condition, uncomplicated preparations, and savory combinations that emphasize the essential qualities of each ingredient are the hallmarks of this rising new cuisine. Along with our willingness to eat new foods comes a fascination with the making of them. Concern with what goes on in the kitchen soon leads us into the garden, for when we begin paying attention to the quality of our foods, we start to wonder where they come from. The more we appreciate distinctive foods, the more we acknowledge and respect the processes of food raising. What begins as perhaps a somewhat narcissistic care for our bodies ends in stewardship for the earth itself.

Our gardens are also a lot more fun than they used to be. Fresh attitudes, fresh ideas and fresh plants lead us in new directions here as well. No longer content to copy European or Asian traditions, Americans are experimenting, combining standard garden elements in unorthodox ways, evaluating the archetypes with fresh eyes. Not afraid of color, not afraid to break with tradition, Americans are willing to try new patterns, to risk making mistakes. Our approach is flexible, curious, a bit outrageous. Homogeneity is no longer a goal; we are recalling our roots, reinventing them if necessary. Regional patterns, regional tastes, regional specialties are valued as never before. We are looking at where we've been, seeing where we are now, eager to move ahead.

We stand on the edge of new things, in gardens yet to mature, coming into our own after long years of uncertainty. In the New American Garden, as young and raw as the New American Kitchen, herbs both savory and beautiful are finding their rightful place. No longer confined to herb ghettos, herbs are incorporated into the complex and still-developing American Border. What their eventual role will be, no one can yet say. The only certainty is that herbs will find new respect there, praised and prized as never before. Beyond that, nobody can say, but the eventual results are sure to be exciting, surprising and well worth the wait. After all, anything may happen when gardeners are pleased to grow edible herbs purely for their looks while seasoning our salads with flowers. ❦

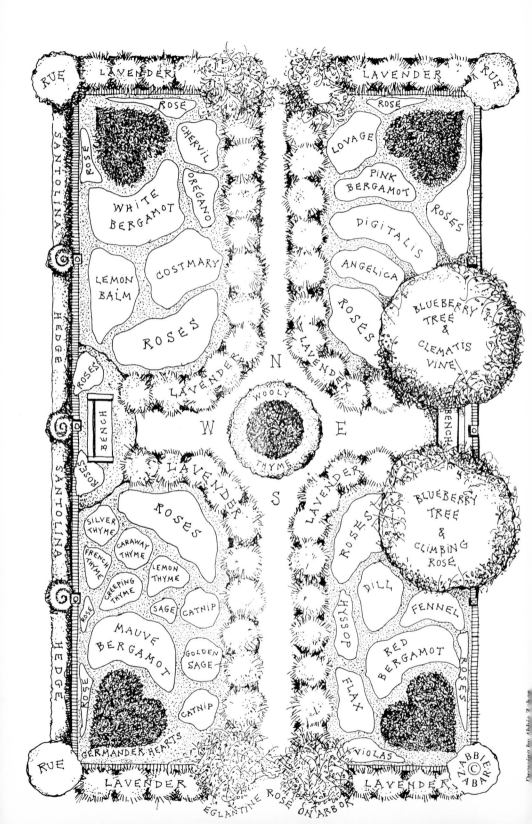

An Elizabethan Herb Garden in A Seaside Meadow

Scented plants inspire dreamers and those who garden on the weekends.

Abbie Zabar

My formal herb garden grows in a seaside meadow, cloistered by Nantucket's scrubby vegetation. It is geometrically precise, yet utterly romantic, incongruous, but logical. It is an evocative 16th-century design that appeared by chance, a folly to satisfy my need for poetry and order in gardening.

Most herbs grow naturally on wind-swept and sun-baked terrains. They thrive in poor soils and with little cultivation. Indeed, herbs are fit and inspiring plants for dreamers like myself, who are limited to weekend gardening.

All through the winter of 1982, my horticultural reading led to medieval and Elizabethan herb gardens. I drew planting plans, fence constructions and gate designs. The following July, a friend and I chose the site,

Abbie Zabar lives and gardens in New York City and on Nantucket. She is the author of The Potted Herb.

Plan for the author's garden drawn before the actual construction began. The 30-by-40 foot space was prepared and surrounded by a handmade, traditional New England fence. The garden was planted in the spring of 1983.

cleared the land and double dug the sandy soil. That is easier said than done. The tangled overgrowth had become a naturalized ambush. There were thorny brambles, brittle underbrush and gnarled vines of poison ivy that had grown as thick as tree trunks.

By Thanksgiving, the house was closed for the season and we had cleared an area larger than the 30-by-40-foot space that would be the herb garden. A top dressing of manure and organic fertilizer was rototilled into the now exquisitely friable soil. The tilled earth looked like a lunar landscape as it was left to winter under a blanket of snow.

In the early spring of 1983, a local cabinet-maker enclosed the garden with a delicate, traditional New England fence. The narrowly spaced pickets created a rhythm of graceful garlands with their pointed arrow tops. The fence was left unpainted to become a weathered gray, so it would not be a visual barrier.

The orderly layout and axial arrangement of my plan is based on the form of a cross and recalls the classic arrangements typical of

Reprinted with permission from The New York Times, *1989.*

ancient gardens. Historically, the cross channels represented four rivers of life that watered the Garden of Eden as well as the four corners of the Earth. Because water is such a central theme of gardens in Persia and India, the name *Chahar-Bagh*, which means a fourfold garden, is still common there. The theme of the four rivers of life is a powerful image that appears in myth, legend, poetry and art throughout Europe and Asia Minor.

Intersecting paths made of pea-pebble divide my garden into north, south, east and west quadrants. I enjoy working with the sun at my back as it circles the sky. Although a fountain or wellhead in the center would have been symbolic, this could not be a feature, as no irrigation or sprinkler system was built into the garden. In fact, for the first years, and until the plants were established, I resorted to a maze of crisscrossing hoses.

The herb garden was planned around boxwood that came from an old New England estate. This shrub has an important horticultural tradition because of its evergreen beauty and finely grained hardwood. Besides, it is easy to prune. At one time, no garden was considered complete without boxwood hedges or topiaries. It was often considered an herb and, as such, boxwood was used as a border in early herb gardens. According to legend, a planting of boxwood guaranteed long life, prosperity and a happy marriage.

My garden was sited by a pair of century-old blueberries that had grown into nine-foot trees. Two teak benches, inspired by a garden seat at Sissinghurst, were imported from England and marked the ends of the garden's north-south path. One teak bench was placed under a canopy formed by the blueberries, the only respite of shade, while the other was put in full sun. That bench was surrounded by pale green canes and alabaster buds of the White Rose of York.

Plantings of 'Hidcote' and 'Munstead' lavender define the walks and enclose the quadrants filled with drifts of gray-green herbs, the color of Nantucket itself. Lemon-scented balm and hairy hyssop, with its beautiful blue-star flowers, attract the neighborhood bumblebees and butterflies.

Lovage is there for its essential Englishness and because its height carries the eye vertically on an otherwise flat terrain, as do the spires of foxglove and stalks of angelica. Sweet woodruff grows under the bench.

Seven varieties of thyme, including a center mound of matted woolly thyme, ring the boxwood. The four quadrants have a different colored flowering bergamot from scarlet red to dusty mauve in bloom from June to September. Feathery leaves of dill and fennel support umbels of little flower heads, while dainty lacelike foliage of chervil barely shades the small gray-green leaves of oregano that creep along the sandy soil on thin purple stems. The flat, wide decorative foliage of ancient costmary brings to mind its former use as a bookmark.

Of course, there are some billowy mounds of small-leaved catnip for my furry four-legged friend Timothy, who visits me in the cool of late afternoon just around his dinner time. Sixty-six bushes of classic roses with names like 'Félicité et Perpétue', 'Maiden's Blush', 'Madame Hardy', 'Autumn Delight', 'Wind Chimes' and 'Reine des Violettes' fill in the garden spaces and weave the fence. Canes of the sweetbriar rose, the Eglantine, whose leaves smell of ripe apples, entwine the arbors that are the east and west entrances to the garden.

Outside the garden and along the fence, a miniature hedge of santolina flourishes in southerly sun. Its cool glaucous color is a refreshing reminder of the nearby foam of ocean waves. It is one foot high and 40 feet long, and is rhythmically punctuated by topiaried cones of santolina. While I designed it to mimic the classic cypress hedges that surround Mediterranean villas, I recently learned that the French once referred to this decorative and aromatic herb as *petit cyprez*. And because rosemary is not hardy in this zone, a pair of potted topiary standards become seasonal sentinels for the entry gate.

CULINARY HERB GARDENS

Rosalind Creasy

What a luxury it is to have a garden full of herbs! Even this country's best chefs usually can't match the meals created from such a garden. Imagine having enough lemon thyme or fennel to be able to use the prunings for smoking pheasant or salmon. Think of creating a salad, as if from the heart of France, with fresh tarragon and chervil, or making an elegant plate of sushi with the traditional *shisho* leaves. Fresh herbs are the signature of a chef and often a specific cuisine, yet very few markets in this country offer more than a meager selection.

When I think back on my cooking of years ago, I seem to myself to have been working in black and white and monaural. The form was there and it was enjoyable, but the depth and richness were missing. Now that I

regularly use fresh herbs, I'm cooking in full color and stereo. The zip of fresh mint or the many flavors of thyme give the dishes more dimension. Twenty years ago, I started on my herb adventure by adding fresh chives to potato soup and fresh basil to spaghetti sauce. What a difference! I went on to use fresh dill

Rosalind Creasy, who lives and gardens in Northern California, is America's foremost proponent of the edible landscaping movement. Her books include the bestselling The Complete Book of Edible Landscaping *and most recently* Cooking From The Garden.

Herbs are the easiest to grow of all edible plants. They are also a healthful way to add excitement to meals. Growing together here are two kinds of parsley and dill combined happily with calendulas in the rear.

9

on fish, pesto on pasta and herb vinegars on salads. Now after years of exposure to the full range of herbs, and thanks to many people's guidance, I use many more in my cooking, and almost all of them are fresh.

Herbs are the easiest to grow of all the edible plants. Another incentive is the fact that cooking with herbs can be a very healthful way to add excitement to meals. At a time when the safety of the salt and fats in our diets is being seriously questioned, it's a relief to explore enjoyable substitutes for them. I get so tired of being deprived in the effort to be "good." Using herbs is a way to deepen the pleasure as well as the healthfulness of food.

Growing Herbs

Variability aside, herbs are among the easiest plants to grow. The majority are perennial plants that need six to eight hours of sun daily, very well drained soil, little fertilizing and some spring pruning for renewal. In areas of the country where the ground freezes they need mulching, and in arid areas summer watering. Tender herbs such as rosemary, lemon grass and lemon verbena must be brought inside in the winter in cold climates; alternatively, these tender perennial herbs can be treated as annuals and replanted every spring. As a rule, herbs are seldom targeted by pests and diseases. Herbs in the South are the exception, and there, where plants are bothered by fungus or nematodes, new perennial herbs can be planted every year in a new area of the garden or in containers. Where garden soil is poorly drained, containers are also the solution; an alternative is planting in raised beds. In most cases, there are solutions to any cultural problem that might arise with herbs, and even gardeners with no yard at all can grow a few herbs on a sunny windowsill.

The annual herbs, such as basil, dill, chervil and cilantro, are grown in a somewhat different manner, as they need annual planting and better soil than the perennials. Give these herbs fairly organic soil and moderate amounts of fertilizer and water. Chervil and cilantro grow better in cool weather and are short-lived plants. For a constant supply, reseed the beds every few weeks as you would for radishes.

Herb plants can be planted in a simple dooryard cluster, in a flower border, in containers or in a traditional formal knot garden. As a rule, because they need similar growing conditions, annual herbs are at home in a bed of annual flowers and/or vegetables or clustered together. Perennial herbs grow best surrounded by other perennial flowers and herbs. For ease of maintenance, the informal cluster of perennial herbs is hard to beat. On the other hand, if a formal knot garden has always been your dream, be prepared to give continual care, as the plants will need constant clipping to look their best. Whatever your choice regarding garden design, the most important factor concerning your herb garden is how close it is to the house. All the herb authorities I know agree that the closer your herbs are to the kitchen door the more you will use them in your cooking.

Harvesting Herbs

For the average cook, harvesting herbs means a last-minute dash to the garden to pick a few leaves for flavoring. Harvesting larger amounts for preserving involves choosing a time when the herbs are at peak flavor and the plants are growing well enough to renew themselves. For the most flavor, harvest most herbs just before the plants start to flower. Another good time to harvest a large amount is when the plants need to be cut back so they can renew. A wonderful way to use large amounts of leftover prunings is for smoking. When you smoke fish or meat, place branches of green herbs such as thyme, lavender, fennel, rosemary or dill over the wet wood chips before you close up the smoker.

Preserving Herbs

Fresh herbs are best, of course, but not all herbs are available year-round, so good cooks over the years have learned ways to preserve the flavors. The best ways to preserve herbs are in oil, in vinegars and by freezing. Another time-honored way to preserve some herbs is by drying.

The following directions for drying herbs can be used for borage, marjoram, mint, parsley, rosemary, sage, bay, chives, dill, thyme, winter savory and oregano.

Pick the leaves in the driest part of the day. Wash quickly, if necessary, and pat dry. Place the leaves in a single layer on a screen. For quick drying, put the leaves in an oven at a *very* low temperature (104 degrees) for a few hours. If you have more time, place the screen in a warm, dry place indoors, such as a garage or attic, and dry for five to seven days. Stir the leaves once a day. When they are dry, store in airtight containers in a cool, dark place.

Cooking from the Herb Garden

I have an amber jar of magic in my refrigerator. It's a marinade of olive oil crammed full of slices of garlic and fresh basil leaves. When I add a spoonful of this oil to an omelet or a soup I feel like Tinkerbell spreading magic dust. Presto! The dish explodes with flavor. Everyday food becomes instant decadence. Actually, *decadence*, with its negative connotations, isn't really the word, since by using this mixture instead of butter I dramatically cut down the amount of cholesterol in the dish. I spread this flavored oil on toast or in the pan before I cook a cheese sandwich. I use it with a baked potato, in a salad, or on green beans and zucchini. Preparing that little jar took, at the most, ten minutes of my time. I picked and sliced a cup of basil leaves, sliced eight or ten cloves of garlic, found a jar, put the basil and garlic in it and poured olive oil in to cover. Sometimes I make the marinade with 'Lemon' basil or 'Cinnamon' basil. I'm sure I could make it with lemon thyme or tarragon, too. No matter which herbs I use, after a week or so of letting the flavors blend, I have a half-pint of pleasure waiting for me in the refrigerator.

How did I ever cook before I learned to make this mixture?

Like most Americans, I grew up with few herbs in my food, and the ones I did know were dried. According to French chef Tom McCombie, ''We Americans are so used to seeing our herbs labeled 'Schilling' or 'McCormick' that we expect them to be grown in the cans we buy them in. Most of us have no idea that basil and tarragon in their fresh form bear no resemblance to the dried products. In fact, most of our cookbooks call for 'tarragon or parsley' and 'chervil or parsley'. Well, they're all green, but that's really where the resemblance ends. In France, I worked in some of the greatest restaurants and I never once saw a can of herbs. I feel that's one of the main reasons French food is so good.''

I know now that I grew up not color blind but ''herb blind.'' And in doing research for my books I discovered that cookbook publishers have unknowingly helped to perpetuate this problem in our society by discouraging authors from calling for fresh or unusual herbs in their recipes. Editors have seemed to assume that listing ingredients unavailable in markets would frustrate their users. This assumption is currently being challenged dramatically. The new chefs writing cookbooks refuse to knuckle under and are, in fact, creating a demand to which stores are responding. And, of course, more cooks are finding that most herbs are very easy to grow.

Pheasant Supremes with Honey and Fresh Thyme

The stock and sauce for this dish are prepared in advance, and the actual cooking of the pheasant takes only a few minutes. The pheasant breasts come straight to the table warm, perfectly cooked and oh-so-easy to eat. Candlelight is recommended.

It is often easiest to bone the pheasant breasts the evening before serving and let the stock makings simmer very slowly overnight. That way, only 20 or 30 minutes' worth of work is left on the way to the grand event.

Pheasant Supremes

Makes 2 large supremes; if thighs used (see below), serves 4.

1 pheasant, 2¼-4 pounds, cleaned and drawn
2 to 3 tablespoons butter, unsalted
2 tablespoons honey
2 teaspoons thyme leaves, fresh
Salt and pepper

Carefully cut breasts from pheasant and remove "tenderloin" strip from back of each supreme (a "supreme" is half of the breast). Skin supremes, dry and wrap in waxed paper while you make rich pheasant stock from carcass (see below). (If desired, debone pheasant thighs and prepare in a similar manner. They will take about twice as long to cook as supremes.)

Ten minutes before serving, salt and pepper supremes on both sides. Melt butter in pan. Sauté skinned side of supreme for 1 to 1½ minutes over moderately high heat until nicely browned. Turn supreme and cook another minute. Cover each supreme with a light coat of raw honey and sprinkle thyme leaves evenly over surface.

Cook until done but still pink in the center, 2 to 5 minutes longer, depending on size. (To check for doneness, press your index finger on thickest portion of supreme from time to time while it cooks. From experience you'll learn to feel when it's done—the meat will offer resistance and spring back. First time around, though, you'll probably want to make a small knife cut and peek inside.) *Do not overcook.*

Cooked supremes can be kept warm for a *few* minutes on a plate set in a warm oven. Don't leave pheasant in sauté pan or it will overcook.

Serve whole supremes on warm plates and top with honey-thyme sauce (see below). Sprinkle on a few more thyme leaves if necessary. Accompany with a seasonal root vegetable.

Lemon grass is a tender perennial grass that will not survive winters in northern climes. It can be brought inside or alternatively treated as an annual and replanted each year. This specimen is planted in a container and over-wintered indoors.

Rich Pheasant Stock

½ yellow onion, diced
1 pheasant carcass after supremes and thighs have been removed
½ bottle dry red wine
Water as needed
½ carrot, chopped coarsely
4 juniper berries
3 peppercorns
1 bay leaf
1 sprig thyme
3 sprigs parsley

Stir onion around on the bottom of a hot stock pot. Chop pheasant carcass into medium-size pieces and add to pot. Stir and turn pheasant pieces to brown them somewhat.

Add wine; then add water until liquid barely covers pheasant pieces. Add all other ingredients and simmer covered for at least 3 hours, skimming surface occasionally and adding more water as needed.

Remove bones and strain stock into clean pot. Skim off layer of floating oil. Bring stock to boil and reduce volume by ⅓. If using later, cool and store covered in refrigerator. Remove thin layer of congealed fat before using for sauce.

Honey-Thyme Sauce

Makes 1 cup.

⅓ teaspoon thyme leaves
¼ cup honey
¼ cup red wine vinegar
½ cup rich pheasant stock, concentrated (see above)
1 teaspoon salt
Pepper to taste

Add thyme to honey and cook over moderate heat until honey turns dark and begins to caramelize. Add vinegar and mix well. Add stock and simmer at very low heat for 15

minutes to blend flavors. Add seasoning. Serve warm over pheasant.

Tulip, Crab and Asparagus Appetizers

This dish is so beautiful it's absolutely eye-popping. And the whole thing, including the petal, is edible. I've used 'Red Emperor' tulips, but you can try any variety that has large, cup-shaped petals. As for the crab, use fresh or frozen, thawed; use canned, drained, only as a last resort.

Makes 25 to 30 appetizers.

3 ounces cream cheese, softened
2 teaspoons lemon juice
1 tablespoon minced chives
1 teaspoon minced fresh dill or mint (optional)
Dash of pepper or cayenne
1 cup (about 5 ounces) crab meat, flaked
25 to 30 fresh asparagus spears
25 to 30 tulip petals

In a medium bowl, beat cheese with lemon juice, herbs and pepper; stir in crab.

Break tough ends off asparagus. Blanch in 1 inch of boiling water in a large skillet with a lid, or steam standing upright in a couple of inches of water in a tall, narrow pot until

Lettuce leaves alternate with leaves of basil in a decorative covering for a bowl containing tabouleh salad. The leaves also complement the taste and texture of the salad.

crisp-tender, 2 to 5 minutes, depending on thickness of stems. Plunge into an icewater bath for 1 minute; then pat dry. Trim asparagus to about 5 inches; from the trimmings, cut as many ¼-inch-thick rounds as you have tulip petals. Save extra ends for salads.

Fill each tulip petal with about ½ a rounded teaspoon of crab mixture and garnish with an asparagus round. (If your petals are large and asparagus thin, you can use 3 rounds to garnish each filled petal.) Arrange asparagus in a fan on a serving platter and place tulip petals alternately (or create your own pattern).

Lavender Vichyssoise

Vichyssoise is an elegant but easy first course. Make it with blue potatoes and you'll really delight your guests. To get the lavender effect, you need to use the very deep purple varieties rather than the medium- or light-blue potatoes carried by some seed companies. The lighter-colored ones will give you a gray, not lavender, soup. The lavender vichyssoise, garnished with chives and chive florets, looks lovely in glass bowls.

Serves 6.

2 tablespoons butter
3 cups sliced white part of leeks, preferred, or 2 cups chopped white onions
3 cups chopped deep-blue potatoes
3 cups chicken broth
1 cup half-and-half
Salt and pepper to taste
Dash of nutmeg
Fresh chives and their flowers, if available, for garnish

In a large saucepan, melt butter and sauté leeks or onions over medium heat to soften but do not brown. Add potatoes and broth; cover and simmer until potatoes are tender, 15 to 20 minutes. Add half-and-half and seasonings and purée in a blender or food processor. Chill and serve cold garnished with chives and chive flowers (separate florets and sprinkle on soup).

Barbecued Vegetables

One of the tastiest ways to prepare summer vegetables is a quick and easy adaptation of the ever-popular barbecue. Although meat, fish or poultry can be a nice complement, the vegetables are so good cooked this way one is tempted to dispense with the rest.

If you are limited by the size of your grill you may have to do a couple of batches. Also consider that the eggplant needs a slightly longer cooking time than the squash and onions, and that the peppers need the least cooking time.

Serves 4.

1 cup olive oil
2 cloves garlic, crushed
¼ cup minced fresh basil or 1 tablespoon minced fresh rosemary
2 medium to large eggplants, cut into ½-inch-thick slices
2 to 4 variously colored summer squash, depending on their size (if large, slice diagonally in ½-inch-thick slices; if small, slice lengthwise in halves or leave whole)
4 small red onions, whole, or 1 large onion, quartered
2 to 4 sweet red or yellow peppers, halved and seeded

In a jar or small bowl, mix oil, garlic and herbs and let stand at least 2 hours (refrigerate if left to stand much longer). Place vegetable slices on a cookie sheet and brush with seasoned oil. Prepare barbecue, and when coals are ready spread them evenly and place vegetables oiled-side down on grill. Brush top sides of vegetables with oil and turn when first side is just starting to brown. Cooking time will vary in accordance with heat, distance from coals and size and density of vegetables. Over medium coals, expect average cooking time to be approximately 4 minutes on the first side and 3 minutes on the second side, but watch carefully. Cook until just tender; if overcooked, vegetables will fall apart. ❧

Gardens To Savor

Simple or Stately, Every Yard Deserves an Herb Garden

Ann Lovejoy

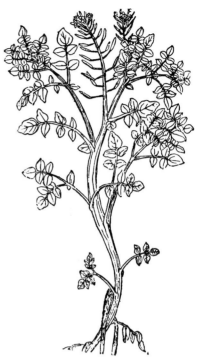

Watercress

It's hard to stay indoors when spring begins to bubble in our veins, and with all the best of intentions toward spring cleaning, we are apt to find ourselves outside at the first sign of sun, poking absently in the newly warm earth, clearing away tired leaves from the firm little snouts of emerging bulbs. Cluttered closets will simply have to wait, for warm washes of thin spring sunshine and light winds carrying the scent of the waking earth lure us willy-nilly into the garden. Even if we have no garden, they are very apt to lure us to the garden center where we can buy far too many little six packs of bedding annuals.

This year, when the gardening itch sets in, make sure your nursery list has plenty of herbs on it, along with all those willing bloomers. Gardenless city dwellers whose plots consist of pots and half barrels ranged on a narrow deck high above roaring city traffic can still grow a wide range of fresh herbs to enliven summer meals and lend their fragrance to summer nights. As long as you can offer plenty of light, water and good garden soil, your herbs will flourish, even where reflected heat and wind make life hard for more delicate border or bedding beauties. Most herbs are native to some pretty tough territory, and they thrive in mediterranean conditions.

Don't feel you must grow your herbs in splendid isolation, for by and large they are excellent mixers. Simply because they are usually confined in herb ghettos doesn't mean that they deserve such treatment; herbs add cooling splashes of gray, silver and blue foliage and complex, lovely textures to typical bedding plantings. They are all fragrant, as pleasant to the nose as roses and violets (both of which may be considered culinary herbs). Herbs are incorporated, often purely as decorative elements, into some of the most sophisticated border schemes in the world. Grand or minute, gardens on every scale are improved by the addition of kitchen herbs, and it doesn't hurt the reputation of the local chef, either.

Those who garden on balconies might consider hanging a plant panel up one wall. These are flat-backed containers made of mesh or wire, stuffed with peat moss and filled with soil mix. Starter plants can be tucked between the wires to create a floral tapestry, taking advantage of available vertical space where ground space is limited. A sunny wall could play host to an arrangement of strawberries, lemon thyme, curly creeping marjoram and honey-scented sweet alyssum,

Herbs and salad greens planted together in pots not only look attractive but can be moved around or out of the way when depleted. Nasturtiums add color to any combination and serve as edible garnishes in salads or other dishes.

with occasional tufts of miniature curry plant, *Helichrysum angustifolium* 'Nana' for contrast. A big terra cotta pot of dill, or bronze fennel edged with purple sage and blue rue would make a distinguished and practical underplanting.

Large containers or tubs can hold small salad gardens of ruffled lettuces, fern-leafed salad burnet, sorrel, chervil and chives. Run a pea net or some trellis up the wall behind your tub for scarlet runner beans, or meltingly tender purple-podded stringless beans, mingled with fragrant sweetpeas. Let mats of thyme and prostrate rosemary tumble over the sides of your barrel, and leave room to tuck in a few pots of basil. Greens and herbs that are quickly depleted can be planted separately, sinking them, pots and all, into the big container. When you use up a plant, pull out the pot and drop in its replacement, reseeding or potting up younger plants to keep a steady supply coming.

Any garden gains from the presence of a trinity of culinary sages: 'Ictarina', variegated gold and green; 'Tricolor', all purply-pink, cream and celadon; and the somber, misty purple sage. The classic, understated 'English Broadleaf', gray and trimly tailored, fits any color scheme, and adventurous cooks will

A strawberry barrel provides a perfect opportunity to plant a pleasing group of herbs in one container. Placed by the kitchen door for convenient snipping are: parsley, rosemary, basil—purple and green leaved, variegated sage and marjoram.

chop it up with rosemary and garlic tips to flavor fresh pea soup, mince it with dill and dijon mustard for fish sauce, or blend it with thyme and marjoram to scatter over veal chops. Add honey, poppyseed and any sort of fresh sage to a wine vinaigrette and splash it over a salad of melon balls and ham.

Fruit salads and cantaloupe are all the better for snippets of aromatic pineapple sage, a plump, matronly creature that takes to the contained life on terrace or deck with panache. Her stalks of clear red flowers are highly attractive to bees, and hummingbirds will squabble and jostle for their lilliputian lion's share of the nectar. The screaming red sages known euphemistically as ''ornamental'' are seldom an ornament to any garden, but the cooler toned blues, whites and silver of the farinaceous salvias, such as 'Victoria' in dark-night blue with white-powdered stems, and the ice pale 'White Bedder', are graceful anywhere. Scads of gray and silvery foliage plants fill out this vast tribe, which is worth thorough investigation.

French tarragon is a lovely, lacy herb with a thousand uses; add a sprig to white wine vinegar and let it steep in the sun for a few days, scatter shredded fresh leaves over broiled or boiled chicken, or snip some into your usual salad dressing. Add chopped tarragon to fresh lemon juice, garlic and olive oil, then marinate swordfish or halibut in the mixture for a few hours before grilling over maple, alder or hickory coals. Sprinkle it, minced, over corn on the cob. Purée a big handful of fresh tarragon with a fat shallot, some walnut oil and white wine vinegar, a bit of orange rind and freshly squeezed juice to make an intensely scented and savory sauce for lamb or lean pork medallions. *Artemisia dracunculus* is the proper name of this creature, and it, too, has a score of ornamental relatives with filigree foliage to add a soothing shimmer of silver to the hot summer garden. Not all of them are quite the thing for salads—they include the bitter herb known as wormwood, and the rather musty one that lends its characteristic flavor to absinthe. Still, all are beautiful, and their leaves have a wild, pungent scent, immediately transporting to those who know the desert.

Gather an armload of basils when you visit a garden center, for they come in several colors and a dozen forms, some exotically scented, all wonderful in the kitchen. For an all-purpose culinary basil, try *Ocimum basilicum* 'Lettuce Leaf', a robust Italian variety outstanding for its big, flavorful

Lamb's ears, Stachys byzantina*, adds a silvery color and texture to a border of mainly green herbs and other perennials. So often the contrasts in color and foliage texture help to point out the unseen attributes of many favorite herbs.*

leaves. 'Purple Ruffles' looks just like it sounds, and is quite easy to grow, unlike other dark-leaved basils. This one is a handsome companion for shrieking pink petunias and looks elegant tucked between arching silver-blue sprays of giant catmint. Thai basil has sharp, spicy overtones, while lemon basil, although it has a marked lemon scent, tastes more of basil than citrus.

For the diet conscious, a savory low-calorie pesto may be made by adding a big scoop of low- or non-fat yogurt to a handful of fresh basil and a few cloves of garlic; buzz in the blender till smooth. If you don't mention the substitution, nobody will ever even notice, and it's great with hot pasta or chilled salads of steamed vegetables. A handful of toasted nuts—whether hazelnuts, walnuts, almonds or the more traditional pine nuts—makes a thicker, richer pesto, and grated parmesan or romano cheese is another tasty, though optional, addition. Add a spoonful of pesto to your usual salad dressing, or put olive oil, garlic and balsamic vinegar in the blender along with a generous handful of fresh basil to make a brisk and aromatic dressing for greens or new potatoes. Since a few rounds of pesto can do in even a good-sized plant, grow basils in small pots that can be pulled out of an ornamental border or a large container garden, where a mangled plant could look less than lovely. Pot up any extras and keep them waiting in the wings as reserves, or replace them with new plants, whether herbal or ornamental.

Basil isn't the only herb for pesto; fine versions can be made using other herbs, too. Try stuffing a whole salmon with a pesto of fresh dill and garlic, or baste a roasting chicken with a pesto of chervil and chives. Lean pork or lamb will stand up nicely to a pesto of fresh fennel and red onion. Use your imagination, and play around with your favorite herbs in combination as well. Those who love *cuisine relevé* will be particularly taken with a pesto of cilantro, the spicy herb that gives its bite to the cooking of South America, China and Asia.

Chervil has a big, bold flavor that definitely does not appeal to some, but the smitten can't get too much of it. To experience this herb to the fullest, purée an entire bunch (washed and trimmed) of fresh cilantro with garlic and a hot chile pepper or two. Thin with olive oil as needed to make a smooth paste, which can be mixed with ricotta and chopped fresh spinach to fill phyllo dough, or blended with sour cream or yogurt for dips. Spread cilantro pesto on a thin dough crust, then sprinkle lightly with grated pecorino and mozzarella; bake this in a very hot oven for an unforgettable pizza.

There are few plants more striking than a huge pot full of well-grown finocchio, the bulb-forming sweet fennel adored by the Italians. In early spring it is among the first plants to appear—a foaming fountain of lively green froth. By summer it becomes huge and architectural, with great feathery arms of finely dissected foliage. In fall it is a tower of soft copper and gold. Each tiny leaf will hold a shimmering drop after a rain, when any stray sunbeam can suddenly set the whole plant aglow. The Italians favor braised fennel with cheese sauce, a combination I personally find disgusting. For my money fennel is born to be sautéed with baby zucchini, pattypan squash and crisp young beans thinly sliced on the diagonal. The leaves may be strewn over grilled fish steaks or sliced tomatoes with equal felicity. They will also grace a salad of leeks and slim, waxy yellow finn potatoes dressed with a mustardy vinaigrette.

Travelers in France will recognize the tart, tangy flavor of sorrel as a common one in French spring salads. The French deserve credit for elevating sorrel from a rank, wrenchingly sour weed into a gastronomic triumph. Young sorrel leaves are wonderful chopped into salads, tuna or chicken sandwich filling, and soups of tiny early vegetables. Sorrel can be sautéed until limp, then blended with crème fraiche and a few green peppercorns and tucked into a light, puffy omelet. An astonishing spring soup can be made by melting the sorrel in butter over gentle heat until soft, adding scalded milk (which will promptly curdle) and buzzing it smooth in the blender. Return the soup to the pan, add lots of cooked shrimp and thinly sliced green onions, then crumble in some crisply cooked bacon. Garnish this with sour cream and lots of freshly ground pepper.

A handful of lemon balm makes a delightful tea, hot or iced, and the finely chopped leaves are a refreshing addition to mixed green or fruit salads and cold soups. Chop a few leaves of lemon balm and mint together and freeze them into your ice cubes to freshen up frozen lemonade or instant iced tea. Planted in the ground it earns a bad reputation for rampant spreading, but in pots, its rowdy ways are checked. A form with warm yellow leaves, called 'Allgold', has better manners and the same appealing fragrance. Try planting 'Allgold' in the front of a potful of dusky red 'Rubine' brussels sprouts with purple sage and golden thyme, or give a big clump an underplanting of variegated mint with leaves shaded in cream and tender jade green.

Mint, though highly ornamental, is another vigorous, not to say flagrant runner that is best confined to pots. Mints are indispensable for enlivening everything from juleps and fruit soups to fresh chutneys and raitas. Some hot summer night when appetites are depressed, grate up a cucumber, drain it for a minute or two, then stir it into a dish of yogurt. Squeeze in a clove of garlic and add a handful of minced mint leaves. The result is a raita, an Indian side dish that makes an enticing addition to midsummer meals. Serve it with cold chicken or grilled fish, or spoon it over a salad of artichoke hearts, fresh mozarella and walnuts, all tucked into split pita bread rounds.

Mints, like basils, come in various sizes and scents; apple mint or pineapple mint, orange mint or coconut-flavored and the curious 'Herba Barona' that smells of caraway and roasting beef are but a few of them. Everybody knows about mint tea, but plain spearmint, uplifting as it is, isn't the only game in town. On cool summer mornings before the sun is fully up, take the teapot with you as you wander through the garden. You can develop your own wake-up blend of mint tea by adding a sprig of several mints, a spray of lemon balm and a few jasmine flowers. Later in the season, combine orange mint, spearmint and mashed, ripe rosehips for a tangy, sweet-tart brew. To make any sort of herb tea, put a handful of herbs—perhaps a quarter of a cup, loosely packed—per person into the teapot. Cover with boiling water and steep for three or four minutes. Strain, and serve plain or with honey.

Few people ever buy chives for this ubiquitous herb lines garden walks from one end of the country to the other, and it is one of those beloved garden plants that always gets swapped over the back fence. This is just as well, since its name, *Allium schoenoprasum*, ought never to be attempted out loud, particularly at the local garden center, where the staff is quite likely to gawk at you and call the manager, who will eventually say, with dawning intelligence, "Oh, you mean chives?" Chives make fat, grassy clumps that can be sliced up with an old knife into as many divisions as you need each spring. Once you have it for a few years, you too will be passing bits of it over the fence to new neighbors. The fluffy lavender flower heads add a piquant touch to mixed greens, float in cold summer soups, or decorate potato salad. Even prettier are the delicate, fragrant white umbels of garlic chives (*Allium tuberosum*), the leaves of which add equal snap to salads, sandwiches and omelets.

This summer, look at your herbs with a fresh view. Let the herbs mingle freely with ornamentals of all persuasions to enrich your garden with their fragrance, color and texture. Don't worry if it feels odd to juxtapose bright blossoms with edible foliage; after all, any combination you try is bound to be in unimpeachably good taste.

Herbs by Curbs

Jerry Sedenko

The traditional place for herbs is in a special garden, usually formal in design, where their needs for sun and good drainage can be met. However, once these plants are freed from formal confines, their purely ornamental virtues become more apparent. And their tough constitutions make them naturals for beautifying difficult situations. The chinks in a retaining wall or a steep bank, particularly if the soil is sandy, can be such a situation. Since herbs are generally thrifty plants, even small nooks and crannies are likely spots for them.

One of the least-gardened and most perplexing areas of any urban or suburban situation is that two- to four-foot-wide plot of ground between the sidewalk and the curb known as the parking strip, tree lawn, or parkway. A pathetic patch of grass is the usual fate to befall this stepchild of the garden. Sometimes ivy or another ground cover is planted. But as time goes by the plants look increasingly forlorn, and the frustrated homeowner turns to the Ultimate Solution: paving.

Why not try herbs and like-minded plants as an undemanding and beautiful alternative? First check with the "powers that be" to learn what the local ordinances say about the legal uses of the strip. Existing small trees can be surrounded by beds of lemon or silver thyme and edged with low-clipped hedges of santolina or lavender. Or why not go in for a touch of Sissinghurst Castle and make a thyme lawn, composed of a collection of mat-forming varieties of *Thymus serpyllum*? Woolly thyme (*T. pseudolanuginosus*) makes a soft gray carpet very quickly, and is beautiful between paving squares or stepping stones. The bits that grow over the edges smell delicious when trodden upon. But if

Jerry Sedenko lives and gardens in Seattle. He is a garden designer whose writing has appeared in Fine Gardening *magazine and* New Voices in American Garden Writing.

One of the least-gardened and most perplexing areas of many urban locations is the two- to four-foot wide plot of ground between the sidewalk and the curb known as the parking strip. Photographed here is the author's solution to this problem. Starting from the front: Antennaria dioica, thyme, catmint and a salvia—a pleasant mixture of colors and textures.

Cotinus coggygria *'Royal Purple' has purple
leaves that combine dramatically with*
Artemisia *'Silver Brocade'.*

you wish to make the parking strip truly a
garden, a mixture of herbs and other lovers
of benign neglect is the way to go.

Because this area is an island, you needn't
worry too much about the design. Think of
it as a place to indulge your "I must grow one
of those" fantasies. The reason you can get
away with this is that virtually any combination of herbs you can come up with looks
good. Many herbs have small gray-green
leaves with soft textures, some being down-
right furry. Mixing these with other plants of
similar color but different size leaves creates
an easy variation on a theme. For a really
large scale effect, a few Scotch thistles,
(*Onopordum acanthium*), cardoons
(*Cynara cardunculus*) or mulleins (*Verbascum* spp.) will add variety, particularly
when they bloom with their six-foot spires
and candelabras.

Mid-sized plants to consider are *Senecio* x
'Sunshine' (*S. grayi*), various forms of Scotch
broom (particularly 'Lilac Time' and 'Moon-
light'), and either forms of silverberry (*Elae-
agnus pungens*) or rockrose (*Cistus* spp. and
hybrids), depending on the severity of the
climate.

*Variegated lemon balm provides a back-
ground for the blossoms of a lavender
campanula. Most gardeners have not yet
discovered this pleasing combination.*

For a spiky or vertical line to serve as counterpoint to all that soft texture, consider irises. There are many kinds of irises and iris relatives that thrive in such a situation, from the hardy bearded hybrids, to that charming midwinter bloomer, *I. unguicularis*. Sisyrinchiums of all sorts are good bets, particularly *S. convolutum* (golden-eyed grass), and *S. striatum*, with its upright wands of cream-colored starry flowers. One of the most subtly striking plants for this effect is evergreen oats (*Helictotrichon sempervirens*). It forms two-foot-high hummocks of steel-blue grass blades, topped by graceful, arching seed heads up to five feet high. Investigate some of the other grasses too. A plant that looks like a giant grass but is in reality a lily relative is New Zealand flax (*Phormium*). In mild climates, the colorful smaller varieties provide a strong architectural note. They come in red, glaucous and golden shades, plus all manner of variegations. Lily-of-the-Nile (*Agapanthus* spp.) has tufts of green strap-shaped leaves, and in midsummer sends up two- to four-foot stems topped with large drumstick clusters of rich blue or white bells. The 'Headbourne Hybrids' are the hardiest sort; at least one gardener in the Great Basin buries the bulbs over a foot deep, where they survive temperatures of at least minus 10 ° F.

In the range of 6 to 24 inches high you might try 'Jackman's Blue' rue, sometimes sold as 'Blue Mound', a particularly fine form of *Ruta graveolens*. *Origanum dictamnus* (dittany of Crete), Australian mint shrub (*Prostanthera rotundifolia*) and the smaller rockroses, such as *Cistus* x *skanbergii*, plus some of the shrubby veronicas (*Hebe* spp.), are good bets in mild-winter areas. They are all evergreen, or perhaps ever gray is more apt. Where the climate is less benign, try the variations of sage (*Salvia officinalis*). The common one is a good doer, as is the yellow-edged variant ('Icterina'). However, the purple-leaved and tricolor forms are a bit less beneficent. There is a lovely sort with extra-pale fuzzy leaves which is particularly striking. The lavenders seem particularly suited to an ornamental assortment of herbs, with their varying heights, grayness and color and form of flowers. English lavender (*Lavandula spica* or *vera*) can become a genuine shrub, up to four feet in time, but the dwarf forms, of which there are several, can easily be tucked in here and there or used as edgers. Try 'Munstead', with early lavender-blue flowers, or 'Hidcote', very dwarf, with deep purple flowers. French lavender (*L. dentata*), with its toothed gray leaves, and Spanish lavender (*L. stoechas*), whose flower spikes are topped with inch-long purple or white pennants, are more tender, but are easily propagated from cuttings and worth overwintering indoors. Rosemary (*Rosmarinus* spp.) has many forms, from rigidly upright to six feet to totally prostrate. The latter look beautiful draped over a retaining wall. Many are hardier than might be expected, and the needlelike foliage always looks fresh and healthy. Some types, notably the upright 'Tuscan Blue', have particularly beautiful blue flowers.

All of the wormwoods (*Artemisia* spp.) are beautiful and undemanding, and are among the most charming silvery plants to be found. There are two basic types: those which spread by underground shoots, and those which stay put as clumps or shrubs. In a large space the running types can be used, but they have a tendency to be thugs. Some of the best are 'Silver King', 'Silver Queen', and 'Lambrook Silver', all upright, and 'Valerie Finnis', somewhat of a flopper. The clumpers are represented by that old standby 'Silver Mound' (*A. schmidtiana* 'Nana'). It makes quite a lovely little tuffet of silver threads until it flowers, at which point it definitely looks as if it's stayed too long at the party. *A. canescens*, on the other hand, is far more substantial when it bears its wands of little yellow buttons. Aside from this attribute, it makes the most charming tangle of low, spreading tattered lace. But the best of the stationary wormwoods is the result of a cross between *A. arborescens* and *A. absinthium* known as 'Powis Castle'. This is the ultimate in silver filigree, and its graceful lax habit makes the two- by four-foot shrub all the more winsome. As a bonus, its hybrid origin means it doesn't flower at all, so it looks beautiful all season. A product of the same union called 'Huntington Gardens' is beginning to make its appearance. It's similar, but more definitely upright-growing. Look for it.

The lavender-cottons (*Santolina* spp.) are real workers. The most common is *S. chamaecyparissus*, and its dwarf form, 'Nana'. Left to themselves, they grow into mounds of gray, rough, finely divided foliage, until they flower. Not only are the little button flowers a charmless shade of mustard, but the bushes flop open from the centers rather embarrassingly. If they are closely clipped in May, both these situations can be avoided. Also, with any of the santolinas, after they've been clipped back hard, try placing a "cage" of small chicken wire over the plant. As it regrows through the wire, the wire will be obscured, and you will have a flop-proof plant. This is particularly advisable when using santolinas as dwarf hedges. Other kinds to look for are 'Bowles' Variety', with gray leaves and cool, pale yellow flowers, and *S. virens*, with green foliage and similar sulphur-yellow flowers. Faster growing than *S. chamaecyparissus*, *S. virens* is tolerant of a bit more water, and is even fire retardant, to boot!

No ornamental herb planting is complete without at least one of the catmints (*Nepeta* spp.). The most common, *N. mussinii*, or *N. x faassenii* (there is confusion in the trade), is a real champ when it comes to fast growth and length of bloom. In one season, a two-inch potful can easily spread to 18 inches across and will bloom from April to November. If it flags, cutting it back hard and giving it a dose of water will have it up and blooming again in just a few weeks. For reasons known only to them, cats are particularly fond of this plant. They love to loll about in it. This can wreak havoc if your neighborhood has a particularly dense feline population, despite the sturdy constitution of the plant. One time-tested solution is to place thorny twigs, such as rose or barberry, among

the leaves. There is a larger growing form called 'Six Hills Giant', similar to the common type in every way except size; it can reach two feet, easily double the height of the smaller one.

Under all this herbage should go the many ground-hugging mat formers. The above-mentioned thymes are ideal, as are golden marjoram and pussy toes (*Antennaria dioica*). The pink form of pussy toes is a delight when the clusters of fuzzy little nubbins hover a few inches above the dense, even carpet of half-inch gray leaves. These sorts of humble plants not only put the finishing touches on the picture, but help keep weeds at bay. Remember, if you don't cover the ground, Mother Nature will make every attempt to do it for you, and you might not like her choices.

Here and there it's nice to have a few clusters of bulbs peeking out. All that gray foliage sets off their bright colors to perfection. Also, many bulbs are native to the same regions as herbs and are therefore easy companions. The minor bulbs, such as species crocuses and tulips, muscari and anemones do particularly well, as do the smaller narcissi. They multiply reliably, thriving in the same baking sun and meager soil that are best for herbs. And tufts of bright little bulb blossoms in the early spring are so cheery that their diminutive size is more than made up for.

So, now that you're committed to doing something creative yet practical, how do you do it? First you must get rid of that grass. Soak the soil well, if it is not spring, to get it growing. Then, on a warm day, break out the systemic, non-residual herbicide. There are other non-chemical ways to kill the grass, such as covering it with black plastic for several months, but be aware that no matter what, there will be grass and weed seeds left behind that will germinate. Ideally, till the ground after the grass is dead and water well to force the culprits to appear. Keep after them.

After loosening the soil there will probably be a certain amount of mounding. It means

Lavender-cottons, Santolina *spp., grow into mounds of gray, rough, finely divided foliage. Keep closely clipped in May and the bushes will not flop over and become untidy. The flowers are yellow and buttonlike.*

that there is more air in the soil, which will also cause it to be warmer. Also, excess water will drain better than it did when it was trodden, a condition that is critical for healthy herbs.

Place your plants in a pleasing arrangement. Groups of two or three of a kind will keep things from looking spotty. Space the taller things in a way that will create a rhythm of plant heights. Don't bother to add any fertilizer, unless there's something wrong with the soil. A bit of time release fertilizer placed in each planting hole will help get things off to a good start, and the gradually decaying tilled-in turf will give a little nourishment later. But remember, these plants thrive on a skimpy diet.

A two-inch layer of mulch will insure that any remaining weed seeds have a rough go of it. By the second year your plants should be a soil-covering size, and the battle of the weeds will be reduced to minor skirmishes. Water moderately but regularly for the first several weeks after planting. In the second and succeeding years, supplemental water will be needed rarely if ever, depending on the plants chosen and the climate. In a surprisingly short time, you will have a genuine garden, less demanding and far more beautiful than what was there before. And you're guaranteed to be the talk of the neighborhood. 🌱

Found At Last
Real Oregano

Origanum vulgare, top, is often described as real oregano. However, Origanum heracleoticum, *at the bottom of the photo, is the culinary oregano that has the true pungent flavor.*

Dorothy Hinshaw Patent

My husband and I love Mediterranean food—hearty pastas, spicy moussaka, and other flavorful dishes that call for plenty of oregano. But when I tried to grow my own oregano, I stumbled on an herbal mystery.

First I ordered seeds of *Origanum vulgare*, which the catalogs described as "true oregano." But the plants I grew from them, with their lovely purple flower spikes, neither smelled nor tasted like store-bought oregano. In fact, nobody could taste them at all! After years of ordering "true oregano" seed from different catalogs, and growing out handsome purple-spiked bushes with no flavor, I began to wonder if it was me or my soil.

Bonnie Fisher of Hickory Hollow Herbs in Peterstown, West Virginia, said that the problem was that *Origanum vulgare*, the oregano sold by most seed companies, isn't oregano at all—it's wild marjoram. Culinary oregano is *Origanum heracleoticum* and has white flower spikes and that true pungent flavor. Ms. Fisher grows both kinds, using culinary oregano in the kitchen and the purple flower spikes of *O. vulgare* in herb wreaths. For culinary oregano, she recommended buying plants, not seed.

Dorothy Hinshaw Patent is a biologist who has written numerous science and nature books for children. She is the coauthor, along with Diane E. Bilderback, of Garden Secrets *and* Backyard Fruits and Berries, *both published by Rodale Press.*

"Culinary oregano has a tendency to revert, to be cross-pollinated when it goes into flower," says Sal Gilbertie, owner of Gilbertie's Herb Nursery in Westport, Connecticut, a wholesaler who supplies plants to the National Herb Garden in Washington, D.C. At Gilbertie's each plant is field-tested for fragrance and flavor, and only the best are chosen for cuttings. But isn't there any way to get culinary oregano from seed? "Greek oregano has the oregano flavor," said Gilbertie, "but it's much stronger, sharper—it bites the tongue." He mentioned that there are three subspecies of Greek oregano, but they all have the same pungent flavor.

I started combing the catalogs again, and two years ago, I found Greek oregano listed in the Richter's Herb Seed Catalog, which announced that its seeds were "true oregano, collected wild in the mountains of Greece." Eureka, I thought, this *has* to be the stuff!

That spring, I planted the Greek oregano seeds indoors. They took a long time to germinate and came up sporadically. The germination rate was low, but I didn't despair—I'd gotten six transplants from my experiment. In June, I planted the seedlings in the garden. They survived but grew slowly until mid-July, when things warmed up a bit. (Western Montana, where I live, is a far cry from the Mediterranean!) I found that placing flat rocks around the plants helped them along.

The Greek oregano plants resembled *O. vulgare* in leaf shape only. My specimens were small and grew close to the ground, with their modest stems hugging the soil. The seedlings varied quite a bit in size and form, but they all shared one important trait—leaves which were delightfully fragrant, the way oregano should be!

When fall came, I potted up my herb plants, now about four inches tall, and brought them into my attached greenhouse for the winter. In the spring, I replanted them in the garden, where they produced small, rather loose stalks of white flowers along with their zesty leaves.

I planted more seeds of the Greek type outdoors in midsummer. I plan to keep growing this oregano every year, maintaining some plants as perennials and harvesting others for their leaves. Because of my harsh climate, I have to baby the plants along, covering them in winter (real oregano is not as hardy as the common kind) and planting them in the warmest, sunniest parts of my garden. But, thanks to my determination (and love of a mystery), I'll have my own garden-fresh oregano whenever I need it—found at last!

Seed Sources for Oregano

Otto Richter & Sons, Ltd.
Goodwood, Ontario
Canada LOC 1AO

Johnny's Selected Seeds
Albion, ME 04910

Plant Sources

Hilltop Herb Farm
P.O. Box 1734
Cleveland, TX 77327

The Sandy Mush Herb Nursery
Rt. 2, Surrett Cove Road
Leicester, NC 28748

Sunnybrook Farms Nursery
9448 Mayfield Road
P.O. Box 6
Chesterland, OH 44026

Well-Sweep Herb Farm
317 Mount Bethel Road
Port Murray, NJ 07865

Reprinted with permission. This article appeared originally in Organic Gardening, *September, 1983.*

DOUBLE VISION

Garden Sage
Salvia officinalis

Linda Hillegass

I'm not sure why I have an herb garden. It isn't that I really use the herbs all that much. Oh, the parsley, of course, and the chives, the occasional snippet of black peppermint in iced tea. I did season the stuffing for one memorable Thanksgiving turkey with frosty sage plucked from a half-frozen garden. But I've grown thyme and oregano for a decade without tossing them in a sauce. My garlic chives are glorious, lush in summer and enchanting in fall with their starry blooms. But I've yet to try their leaves among salad greens. I go right on buying those bottled herbs at the grocery store just as if I had no herb garden at all.

The truth is that my herb garden is a sensuous experience that has to do with scent, sight and texture far more than with taste. I love the silvery green of sage as a background for darker colors like the deep green of chives that produce a shower of lilac, cloverlike bloom in spring. My black peppermint mats the ground in a thick, rich and completely satisfying way. When it strays beyond its bounds I enjoy pulling up its pungently scented runners. The drift of aroma from a thyme plant brushed while weeding is earthy and exotic like a fresh wind from Greece.

Linda Hillegass lives and gardens in Lincoln, Nebraska, where she is also co-owner of a bookstore. "Double Vision" is reprinted with permission from New Voices in American Garden Writing, *published by Capability's Books. Her writing has appeared in* Fine Gardening *and* Nebraskaland *magazines.*

I can't think of a part of my garden I enjoy more than my patch of herbs and lately it's become one of my true successes, too. My great love is flower gardening. I spend hours and dollars and sweat on it, but I'm sorry to say that the garden in midsummer seldom lives up to my hopes for it in January. My failures are all too frequent. I've developed a philosophical outlook on these disappointments since taking up garden photography. I begin to see just how the illustrations in garden books can look so lovely. It's all a question of angle, foreshortening and focus. Those seemingly perfect gardens no doubt have their share of gaping holes.

But success is mine in the herb garden, at least since I hit upon the idea of interplanting

The beautiful, green finely dissected leaves of parsley work well with many other plants. The author often mingles spring-flowering bulbs between her herbs.

Photos by Elvin McDonald

bulbs and spring flowers among the perennial herbs. Early in my career as an amateur herbalist, I made the usual mistake of planting too closely. It was a natural error. In spring the gaps around a tiny oregano plant and a pruned thyme loomed large. Closer planting gave the herb bed an established look in May, but later in the season this approach created havoc. Reveling in the sunny site and the heat of a Nebraska summer, the herbs ran riot.

Now among more widely and properly spaced herbs I insert bulbs and other spring flowers to fill the gaps. Their foliage dies away to make room for the vigorous summer growth of sage, oregano and parsley. I've planted daffodils between a well-established sage and a big clump of chives. In early spring, when the daffodils rise along with the temperatures, I prune the sage sharply back to give space to the bulbs. By the time the daffodils have finished blooming the sage has put on new growth and begun to fill in around and over them, hiding their withering leaves.

The plantings, designed to create a spring wave of bloom, give heavy emphasis to daffodils—lovely orchidlike white 'Thalias' and gloriously sunny 'King Alfreds', as well as a few mixed nonentities. Since daffodils return reliably year after year and even increase, they provide a reliable backbone for the garden's early season. The remaining springtime spaces are filled with a sprinkling of tulips, a pair of bleeding hearts (*Dicentra spectabilis*), yellow columbines, perennial gold alyssum, and white candytuft (*Iberis sempervirens*).

The tulips were bought cheap at the drugstore after years of hard luck with expensive tulips which bloomed splendidly one season only to languish a second year and fizzle out completely by a third. The drugstore bargains were to be disposables, bought with the idea of discarding them after a season or two of bloom. Ironically, they have lived on and bloomed lustily for years. They were labeled "mixed," which I took to mean red, purple,

Containers are often the answer to extending the short growing season in northern climes. Combined here to charming effect are: parsley, pansy, English daisy and sweet alyssum.

yellow, pink and so on, but one batch of them came up all white. Planted near the white 'Thalias' they created what I at first regarded as an unfortunate color association. Still I have come to admire this white on white look and enjoy the lovely bridelike bouquets I can cull from this garden in spring, sometimes with the addition of a few branches from a nearby apple tree.

The overall springtime effect of delicate white and yellow blooms with a dash of pink from the bleeding hearts and an accent of red from a few of the tulips is quite breathtaking. Sometime between late March and mid-April this combination bursts into bloom in unison and lasts a few days to a few weeks, depending upon how quickly the hot winds come. The garden appears almost solid with daffodils and their compatriots at this point, the herbs, hardly noticeable.

Tucked up against the stone wall of the garage, with a fence on its southern side, my herb garden has a western exposure that gives it a sunny site while still protecting it from the full blaze of the sun that scorches plants all too easily in a Nebraska July and August. The bed is large—an elongated triangle about 32 by 30 by 12 feet—with plenty of space for a liberal use of bulbs and spring plants that return year after year. Interplanting, though, seems just as suited to a tiny plot outside the kitchen door where, among half a dozen plants of parsley, thyme and chives, one might tuck a few crocuses or species tulips.

After the glory, of course, comes the gore, when the lovely spring bloom dies away, leaving the trashy fading foliage of daffodils, the flopping tulip leaves, the withered bleeding hearts. But this period is not forever. A second wave of bloom in late May and well into June helps to hide the leafy remnants. Yellow columbines and orange poppies set off the blue of Siberian iris and the blue-to-purple range of herbal blossom just coming on: lavender chives, blue sage and purple-blue catmint.

Excepting only the columbines, the gold alyssum, the candytuft, and the Siberian iris, all of these flowers die to the ground shortly after they bloom. The trash withers away, the herbs expand into the holes left behind, and by midsummer I can smugly survey the thrifty, sweet-smelling, bee-busy herb garden which has magically replaced my springtime fairyland. 🌱

The Big Three Herbs For The Home Garden

Parsley
Petroselinum crispum

Doc and Katy Abraham

What are the three best herbs for the home gardener? Here are our favorite candidates:

1. Basil. There are over 40 known varieties of basil. Of all the herbs, basil is one of the easiest to grow and most useful. Start plants from seed indoors, harden off around May and plant 12 inches apart in full sun. Basils prefer a soil high in organic matter. We till rotted leaves into the soil each year to hold moisture in dry weather.

Ocimum basilicum 'Citriodorum' (lemon basil), pale dull green foliage and a strong lemony smell. We like its compact, bushy habit.

O. basilicum (anise basil), purple foliage, white flowers, sweet anise flavor.

O. basilicum 'Crispum' (cinnamon basil), white flowers and a cinnamon flavor.

O. basilicum 'Green Ruffles', white flowers, plus handsome lime-green foliage—an excellent plant in borders or in pots.

O. basilicum 'Purple Ruffles', very showy in annual beds and borders, or in pots. Excellent in vinegar and as a garnish.

O. basilicum 'Purpurascens', deep purple with shiny foliage and lavender flowers. Useful in vinegar and as a garnish.

Doc and Katy Abraham have run a successful commercial greenhouse and landscape business for over a quarter of a century. They teach horticulture at the Community College of the Finger Lakes. They also write a self-syndicated garden column and produce their own radio and TV garden show.

O. basilicum 'Dark Opal', shiny purple foliage, useful in vinegar and as a garnish.

O. gratissimum, yellow-white flowers and gray-green foliage with strong clove scent and spicy flavor.

O. sanctum 'Holy Basil', lavender flowers and a gray-green coarse foliage, sweet fragrance. Highly ornamental but not used in cooking.

Our way to preserve basil:

Wash the leaves and roll them into a cigar shape (while wet) and wrap in aluminum foil. Place in the freezer. When we want to use some, we simply unroll the foil, slice off what's needed and reroll and refreeze the remainder. Loose leaves can be placed in a plastic bag and frozen.

Another method recommended by Nichols Nursery consists of using an equal amount of basil leaves and grated parmesan cheese. Chop basil leaves in a food processor. Stir well with the parmesan and store in refrigerator for two to three days so that the flavors are blended. Great for fresh or cooked tomatoes, salads and pastas. Place in plastic cottage cheese containers to freeze.

Basil can be stored in oil, vinegar or as a frozen paste. Basil can be dried and stored in tightly sealed glass jars.

2. Oregano. *Origanum vulgare.* Order seeds from a reputable seedsman. We start our seeds (very tiny—130,000 per ounce) in Pro-mix (soilless mix). Sow thinly, keep moist and at 72 degrees F. Most oreganos germinate in five days or so. Separate plants into pots and, around Memorial Day, put plants in garden. Harvest the leaves as the plants grow. In fall, we pull up the plants and hang them in our garage to dry.

Home-grown oregano often lacks flavor. Don't start harvesting until flowering begins. Tests show that flowering doubles the concentration of oil in oregano leaves, making them most flavorful late in the season. The opposite is true for nonflowering oreganos in which leaf oil concentration rises steadily in the spring but drops off in fall. Even at their late spring peak, leaf oils in nonflowering plants can't match the autumn levels in flowering oreganos.

3. Parsley. Parsley can be grown as a garden plant, or in the kitchen window all year long. This herb is full of vitamins, high in chlorophyll—a natural breath sweetener. Parsley seed is difficult to germinate, and seedlings difficult to transplant. Always use fresh seed. The seed has a natural inhibitor on the coat so soak seeds in warm water to wash off the chemical inhibitors and hasten germination. If sown outdoors, pour boiling water over the row of seeds before covering. We start our seed in Jiffy Pellets, three or four per pellet, and set out pellet and all. Grow in full sun.

There are two kinds: the flat leaf or Italian parsley (*Petroselinum crispum* 'Neapolitanum') and the curly leaf. The flat leaf has more vitamins, a stronger flavor and is ideal for drying or freezing. The curly leaf type is prettier, tastier. You can use parsley for almost any foods except breakfast cereals and sweets. Digging up a clump of parsley in fall and bringing it indoors in winter is not a good way to start new plants. Parsley has tap roots and so does not transplant easily. Start new plants from seed. To us, dried parsley tastes like hay. We prefer to pull up the stems, wash sprigs and foliage and roll into a "cigar." Wrap with aluminum foil and freeze. It stays green and fresh. ❦

Drying Herbs in the Microwave:

Wash sprigs, pat dry with paper towels. Remove leaves from stems and measure two cups of foliage. Spread evenly on double thickness of paper towel. Turn microwave on high for four to six minutes. Stir several times during drying. When fully dried, herbs will be brittle and will rattle when stirred. Store in fruit jars or airtight containers in a cool, dry place.

Parsley is full of vitamins, high in chlorophyll and pretty to look at. It is easily grown either indoors or out.

Oregano seeds will germinate in five days or so and can be planted out in the garden after Memorial Day. Harvest only after flowering begins for fullest flavor.

Of all the herbs, basil is the easiest to grow and the most useful. There are more than 40 known varieties from which to choose. Start seeds indoors for later planting in the garden.

Please Don't Pass The Salt!

If you're on a low-salt diet, use the three herbs together as a salt substitute.

One mixture consists of two teaspoons of garlic powder and one teaspoon each of basil, oregano, parsley and powdered lemon rind . . . or dehydrated lemon juice. Put the ingredients in a blender and mix well. Add rice to the mixture to prevent caking and store in a glass container.

For a more pungent seasoning, take three teaspoons basil, two teaspoons summer savory, two teaspoons each of celery seed, ground cumin seed, sage and marjoram and one teaspoon of lemon thyme. Mix well, then mash into a powder with a mortar and pestle. To make a spicy seasoning, mix one teaspoon each of cloves, ground pepper and crushed coriander seed, two teaspoons paprika and one tablespoon of rosemary. Mix the ingredients in a blender, then store in airtight container.

ORNAMENTAL HERBS TO SAVOR

Ann Lovejoy

Just as a dash of fresh rosemary or lemon thyme can wake up a workaday salad, so an infusion of herbs brings snap to a humdrum border. We don't have to ransack the specialty catalogs to find good looking, aromatic candidates for such a role; some fine and highly attractive plants are probably blushing unseen in the kitchen garden already. Anybody's list of the choicer salvias will certainly include some of the culinary sorts; the fuzzy gray 'English Broadleaf' sage will slip unobtrusively into any color scheme,

Allium tuberosum, garlic chives, has a grassy sort of growth and appearance topped by flat umbels of sweetly scented white flowers. The blooming plant is rather dramatic.

Bottom left:
Allium schoenoprasum, chives, can be interplanted with other plants for a pleasing effect. The fluffy purple blossoms complement the grasslike foliage.

Anethum graveolens 'Bouquet', dill, has lovely feathery leaves and umbrellalike yellow flowers. Seedlings appear everywhere and can be pulled out where not wanted.

Photos by Elvin McDonald

making stronger colors all the brighter for its quiet presence. Rippling mats of curly golden marjoram make a lovely, close carpet for edging path or border and the golden leaved form of feverfew (*Chrysanthemum parthenium*) refreshes the eye and brightens shady corners as well as it cures migraines and brings a pungent bite to mild salads.

Choosing among the many flowering alliums in the garden catalogs can while away a wet week, but some of the nicest won't even be in the running. Common chives are a lovely foil for *Diascia rigescens*, a long armed twinflower with lipped flowers of a curious metallic pink. Chives can be planted to good effect near one of the hardiest flowering maples, *Abutilon* x *suntense*. The deep, fluted cups of rich lavender are a perfect match for the fluffy purple chive blossoms, and the grassy foliage of the latter looks nice at the shrub's feet. (This abutilon has proved hardy to 5 degrees.) Garlic chives, *Allium tuberosum*, are similarly grassy, if larger overall, but this one opens flat umbels of sweetly scented white flowers that look especially pretty emerging from the skirts of the low polyanthus rose, 'The Fairy' with its muted pink blossoms. The tall, gray-green blades of common culinary leeks have distinct garden presence, and their massive flower heads in faded mauve and cream are architecturally attractive for months after the flowers have faded. The flower stalks droop with age, tumbling companionably into whatever sits in front of them. They look especially nice growing through roses underplanted with masses of oregano (keep 'em guessing), which also holds its seedheads in good condition for months. Alliums are easily grown from fresh seed, though divisions taken from the vegetable patch will have greater garden impact right away.

The many forms of sweet fennel, *Foeniculum vulgare*, are all more or less decorative. Finocchio, or Florence fennel, with a bulbous base and an odd aniselike flavor, has proved perennial in the North-

west, returning placidly after single digit winter lows. Early spring awakens a froth of bright green that elongates into slender stems. These can reach five feet by midsummer, forming shimmering towers of fine, hairlike foliage. Spangled with rain or dew, this fennel sends scintillations of light through the garden. In fall, it passes away in a burst of copper and gold, lovely and aromatic to the very end. A constantly coppery cousin of common fennel is called variously bronze, black, purple or red fennel. The color is a smoky admixture of them all, the olive bronze tones ascendant in shade (which this plant tolerates very nicely), the warm purple-black tints more pronounced in full sun. This is a stunner, especially when grown in a good sized clump. Paired with the red European wood spurge, *Euphorbia amygdaloides* forma *purpurea*, backed by thickets of *Macleaya cordata*, the plume poppy, and given a front row of something silvery like lamb's ears (*Stachys byzantina*) or steel-woolly balls of *Artemisia canescens*, the coppery fennel adds an unmatchable lightness to the textures and tones of its companions.

Most dramatic of all is the European giant fennel, *Ferula communis*. One does not toss its wiry, netted foliage into the salad bowl, but nothing looks fresher than the spumy young shoots of this energetic fennel when they spring eagerly from the cold soil in the last days of winter. It takes several years for a plant to reach maturity, but once established, it will send lusty bloom stalks as much as 15 feet in the air. Each is capped with a well wrapped yellowish knob that splits to reveal a huge, wheeling umbel of coarse white florets. All fennels seed generously and come effortlessly from fresh seed, though the seedlings transplant well only when quite young. If you find lots in the garden, you can transfer tiny clumps to four-inch pots, then grow them on for a bit before setting them in their final spot. Large plants will almost never accept transplanting, but nearly always scatter quantities of seedlings to replenish old stock.🍂

All Herbs Were Weeds Once: Using Native Herbs in Alaska

David Lendrum

S outheastern Alaskans are blessed with a huge, rich, beautiful land virtually un-populated by humans which teems with edible fish, shellfish and wildlife. Far from being the frozen land of igloos and dogsleds, it's much more like the Olympic Peninsula of Washington, with huge trees growing close to the ocean's edge along a glacially sculpted filigree of coastline. Hundreds of small streams run off steep mountains into a sea warmed by the immense Japanese current as it sweeps past glaciers and snow packs, so the marine life thrives as in few other places in our nation. Despite the lack of traditional European herbs, a regional cuisine has de-veloped that is unmatched in variety, with flavors far from those found in the usual North American cooking.

Cuisine is influenced by many factors, including:

availability of ingredients: price, freshness, seasonal reliability and access to shopping areas

regional staples: in our case, the pro-ducts of sea and shore

local agricultural production: totally lacking in Juneau

ethnic derivation of the populace: which in the archipelago of islands and islandlike communities on the mainland leans heavily to Northern European, Japanese and Native Alaskan, with a generous admix-ture of Filipinos, Hawaiians and other Pacific Islanders brought here during the long mari-time trading period.

Long periods without supplies from out-side have caused the Alaskans to look closer to home for the flavorings and colorings that enhance foods—taste, texture and visual at-tractiveness. We do not expect fresh herbs to be available in our corner market, and any larger emporium may be visited only month-ly, so if it can't be grown or gathered locally, it is reserved for vacation trips south or done without.

This should not suggest that our cuisine is bland; it is one of the most exciting in the world, combining Scandinavian, Scottish, Irish, Russian, Filipino and Alaskan native in-spiration with ingredients southern chefs would die to possess. Beginning with sea-food, we dine on four types of salmon, hali-but, cod, Ling Cod, Dolly Varden, trout, crab (Dungeness, Tanner or King), mussels, clams, oysters, abalone, shrimp, prawns, cockles and a host of white-fleshed fish known collective-ly as "bottom fish." Meats are primarily venison, moose, caribou and bear.

Herbs we can grow are greatly restricted, either by the torrential summer rains or by the bone-chilling winter cold that freezes the ocean. The ancient Mediterranean staples of rosemary, thyme, basil and sage are drowned and washed away, so instead we concentrate on parsley, dill, oregano, chervil, sorrel and chives. These northern natives provide flavorings that, if taste were scripted like music, would sing the high notes.

David Lendrum and his wife, Margaret Tharp, own and operate Landscape Alaska, a nursery, landscape and cut flower business in Juneau. Before coming to Alaska, he spent 10 years as the horticulturist for the city of Eugene, Oregon, ran greenhouses at the Carnegie Institute at Stamford and raised fresh market produce in Ecuador. The research for this piece was carried out with the help of a young Tlinkit Indian called the Weed Woman, who introduced the Lendrums to many native Alaskan foods over the years.

Not many traditional herbs will grow in Alaska because of the extremes in weather. Sorrel pictured here is one of the northern natives that will grow and thrive.

The true regionality of our cuisine is provided by the indigenous plants gathered along the ocean's edge or in the woods and marshes that drain into it. These plants are sources of essential vitamins, minerals and fiber, and are real treasure troves of new flavors. Seafood dishes are often accompanied by sea vegetables. These include several edible seaweeds known locally as ribbon, bull or Indian kelp, which have a vegetable texture, taste lightly of the sea and resemble oriental flavors, smooth and delicate. They float in the surf and can be gathered after a storm and dried for use in soups and chowders or steamed back to a moister state and served alongside. Sea lettuce is pulled from the rocks along the beach and served fresh and raw, fresh and steamed, dried and crumpled like pepper, pickled like chow-chow or piccalilli, or marinated in vinegar with onions and cooked carrots. These ingredients provide the savory broth in which the seafood is cooked—not to be forgotten once tasted.

The same gathering trip can yield 10 or 15 pounds of steamer clams and a five-gallon bucket of bull or Indian kelp (use the long leaves, not the hollow, thickened skin). And if you like the spicy flavor of sorrel, it is abundant at the tide line, so gather a couple of quarts of its arrowhead-shaped leaves to steam for a side dish. Steam the clams in a large pot into which the kelp has been chopped and covered with water. When the clams open, serve in a large bowl with a bed of sorrel. The clam juices running into the sorrel leaves will provide all the seasoning.

Another product of the shore is the Indian rhubarb (*Heracleum lanatum*), a huge plant with eight-foot stems and two-foot palmate leaves topped by a inflorescence like a Fourth of July explosion. It has spicy-flavored stems which must be peeled to avoid blisters, but can then be chopped and sprinkled over venison or bear steaks before broiling. These same stems are often blanched and served with leaves of sorrel, dock and yarrow (*Achillea millefolium*) to create a vegetable medley much desired by locals.

Alaska is home to some 25 kinds of edible berries, many in such abundance that native peoples made rakes to gather them, stripping gallons from the waist-high bushes and drying them for winter use. We use these berries as a condiment—cooked into a jam or dried and sprinkled over a moose roast with bay leaves and onions so they plump up during the cooking and make small, sweet drops in the gravy or dressing.

Alaskan cuisine is thus enriched by our lack of traditional herbs. Flavors are where you find them, and they may reside anywhere if you just look. The native people of every region made use of the plants around them for shelter, weapons, medicine, magic, religion and flavoring agents added to all types of foods. We may have carried our ancestral recipes to our new homes, but, just like the scenery, there is something different just over the hill. ❦

Herbs
Southern
Style

Nancy Goodwin

An herb garden can be a splendid thing. But, must you have an herb garden to enjoy herbs? Must those culinary and medicinal plants be forever restricted to the herb garden? Is their survival dependent on it? Is this the only way you, the gardener, can put them to use? Can they serve any function in the garden other than as a source of culinary and/or medicinal ingredients? The answer to all of these questions is "no." There are many reasons you might want to integrate herbs into the rest of the garden. Some are showy enough in bloom and/or leaf to mingle with lilies and phloxes. Others add fragrance to a garden, which although visually pleasing, might otherwise offer little for the sense of smell.

There are many good reasons for gathering all of the herbs into one garden, an herb garden. The convenience of having them all nearby is primary; however, these plants do not occur in herb gardens in the wild, but in complex associations with many other

Salvia officinalis, *sage, has narrow, gray-green leaves and is an attractive addition to a mixed border. The blossoms appear on spikes in early summer and are a violet-blue hue. The flowers often hum with bees.*

plants. They do not all have the same cultural requirements. Those of Mediterranean origin such as lavender, rosemary, the thymes and oreganos, need full sun and sharp drainage, while others such as sweet cicely, angelica and woodruff need some protection from the hot, southern sun and a more moisture-retentive soil. Herbs with different cultural requirements can more appropriately be placed in different parts of the garden—rosemary in that sunny, hot spot at the edge of the driveway and woodruff as a groundcover under azaleas.

Alchemilla mollis, *lady's mantle,* Salvia officinalis 'Tricolor', *alyssum and a small-leaved hosta make an effective combination. Lady's mantle is grown for its lovely foliage that is further enhanced by droplets of water that often bead the edges.*

Nancy Goodwin is the proprietor of Montrose Nursery in Hillsborough, North Carolina, where she grows many unusual perennials. Her specialties are raising hardy cyclamen from seed and educating gardeners to protect natura! populations of endangered plants from over-collection by buying only commercially raised plants.

Giant Mountain Garlic

on which countless butterflies and bees perform. Both of the chives make good cut flowers. Two other alliums which provide interesting architecture rather than colorful bloom are giant garlic and Egyptian topping onions.

Giant garlic, *A. scorodoprasum*, is similar to a leek. Each fall, giant garlic arises from its summer dormancy, producing broad, slightly grayish, straplike and handsome leaves, which persist throughout the winter. In May each mature bulb produces a large bud on a stalk that seems to reach ever higher, eventually topping four feet. The bud is sheathed in a tunic of the same gray-green as the foliage. A cluster of these skyward buds suggests many things: hooded monks or a gaggle of geese with upward pointed bills. Despite their height, these plants are best placed near the front of the border where their personalities make a statement. Their narrow outlines will not hide anything behind them. The sheath is eventually shed

Beyond the fact that it is possible to grow herbs outside the confines of an herb garden, might not some herbs deserve a prominent place for their beauty alone? The answer is "yes" once you recognize those plants which are commonly seen both in and out of the herb garden. Two that come to mind right away—lamb's ears, *Stachys byzantina*, and lady's mantle, *Alchemilla vulgaris*—are likely to be seen in the perennial or mixed border or as ground covers in front of shrubs, especially old garden roses. Lamb's ears are indispensable where silver foliage is desired. Although it doesn't like hot, damp weather, it recovers readily. Herbs such as alliums are ornamental in any garden. The lovely, pink flowers of chives earn them a spot center stage. Cut the whole plant to the ground after it blooms to prevent seeding and to force fresh growth.

Garlic chives, *Allium tuberosum*, are an even better ornamental than the common chive. They flower much later (in late summer) when there is less in bloom and thus are appreciated more. They always stand upright, never becoming sloppy, and their fragrant flower heads of pure white stars are the stage

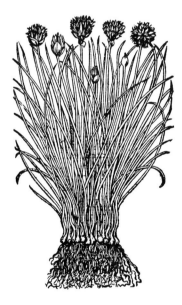

Chives
Allium schoenoprasum

and the resulting flower head is a three-inch-diameter sphere of grayish mauve, which is not unlike the giant purple allium, *A. giganteum*, Dutch bulb dealers try to sell you every year. Although the color is duller, the plants are much more permanent. It is worth growing even if it never opened its flowers. The bulbs can be harvested in summer when they go dormant and they provide a mild garlic flavor when cooked.

The Egyptian topping onions, *Allium cepa* var. *aggregatum*, are those peculiar plants that produce a cluster of little onion bulbs where a normal onion would have its flowers. These bulbs all sprout and the cluster becomes a veritable Medusa's head of green sprouts. Perhaps this sounds too bizarre to use as an ornamental, but it might be just what you need to add a touch of humor to the garden. Imagine a clump or two of these onions piercing a broad, low mass of some self-important bedding plant such as marigolds or ageratum.

Parsley, *Petroselinum crispum*, is as pretty as many ferns and such a lovely, lively green that it can be used as a foliage plant here and there in sunny parts of the garden. Plant enough so you can share some with the green and black celery worms. They are incredibly handsome creatures and the butterflies they become are like flowers that have taken wing.

Two of parsley's cousins, dill, *Anethum graveolens*, and fennel, *Foeniculum vulgare*, have different uses in the kitchen, but have similar uses as ornamentals. Both create an airy, mistlike appearance with their thread-fine foliage. Dill's bright chartreuse flowers brighten up its neighbors, making hot colors appear clearer but not hotter. It is one of the few colors that looks good with those pinky-orange modern roses like 'Tropicana'. Dill is an annual but where happy will reseed and produce several crops each year. The bronze-leaved form of fennel is an especially beautiful perennial herb which combines well with purples or with hot colors.

Basil, *Ocimum basilicum*, has a similarly colored form. The old variety, 'Opal', was always a weak thing but the new cultivar, 'Purple Ruffles', is as robust as it is handsome. The large, purple, ruffled leaves resemble perilla, *Perilla frutescens*, but it is unlikely that it would ever reseed as heavily as perilla does. (Perilla seedlings are easily removed from any place where they are not wanted.) Both of these purple-leaved plants contrast sharply with silver-leaved ones such as *Artemisia* x 'Powis Castle' and *A*. x 'Valerie Finnis'. We would include basil in a garden just to be able to smell it, either on the air when the weather is warm, or when touched. There are many basils with nearly as many different fragrances; lemon, licorice and cinnamon are a few. (By the way, try using pesto as a substitute for the traditional ingredients in deviled eggs. Mix pesto with the hardboiled egg yolks.)

Thymes bring to the garden an even more varied array of fragrance than do the basils. Many thymes succeed in this climate if they have good drainage, which can be improved with the addition of organic matter and grit or gravel. The prostrate thymes are a must between stepping stones where an occasional trodden shoot will release its fragrance. Their flowers add color in their season, but the silver and gold variegation of some thymes add color all year.

Often it is variegation or some variation from the norm that turns a nondescript herb into a garden feature. 'All Gold' is a cultivar of lemon balm, *Melissa officinalis*, which has solid yellow leaves. It is superior to the older cultivar which was merely spotted with gold and would eventually produce solid green shoots. We have used 'All Gold' among coreopsis and gaillardia in a hot color border. The gold-leaved form of oregano, *Origanum vulgare*, could be used in the same combinations, or in a blue and gold border where it is lovely with the blue foliage of rue, *Ruta graveolens*, an echeveria that is summering out of doors, and the gray foliage of the horned poppy, *Glaucium flavum*. The oreganos seem much less fussy about their soil than do the thymes. We have our original

Garlic chives, Allium tuberosum, *has delicate white flowers that appear in late summer. The fragrant flowers attract bees and butterflies. The flowers can be cut for arrangements as well.*

golden oreganos after eight years. There are the purple, golden and tricolor forms of sage, *Salvia officinalis,* but they are difficult to grow unless given perfect drainage. It is best to start new ones yearly by taking stem cuttings before the original plant dies.

Ornamental grasses are enjoying great popularity now. Two important herbs which are grasses and gorgeous are lemon grass, *Cymbopogon citratus,* and vetiver, *Vetiveria zizanioides.* Both are tender and need to be overwintered in a frost-free cold frame, greenhouse or windowsill. Both offer the delightful, airy texture typical of other ornamental grasses. Vetiver is so tall and narrow, at least when young, that it can be used almost as an exclamation point among lower plants, or a fountain perhaps, as grasses are so often described. Lemon grass is shorter and is one of the few grasses with grayish foliage. It is a delightful addition to a planting of silver- and gray-leaved plants because its texture is different from most of the other plants.

If all of the preceding plants find a role outside the herb garden because they are ornamental, we want to encourage the addition to the ornamental garden those plants which might be considered plain, dull or even ugly but which bless us with delightful fragrances. Anise-hyssop, *Agastache foeniculum,* isn't ugly, although its appearance is somewhat

dull, but we would never want to be without it. The fragrance of a crushed leaf is as bright and refreshing as a tall, cool glass of sarsaparilla. We buried our noses in this plant while gazing upon the scentless alstroemerias or Siberian irises: any garden becomes a fuller experience as more and more of the senses are involved. Even weeding is made more pleasant when working among fragrant plants.

Plants that should definitely escape the herb garden are those that never really belonged there in the first place. Often they have no herbal uses themselves but are relatives of herbs. To be used only in the herb garden is perhaps a little like having one's occupation restricted to that of one's greatuncle once-removed. Three genera that come to mind are *Salvia, Allium* and *Origanum.* The alliums include garlic and onions. *Salvia officinalis* is the culinary sage and Origanum is oregano and marjoram. All three of these genera include many non-herbal but showy members that should be better known by gardeners. Some wonderful salvias such as Mexican bush sage, *Salvia leucantha,* the hybrid *S.* x 'Indigo Spires' and *S. greggii* have just begun to receive the attention they deserve. *Origanum pulchellum* is one of the many ornamental oreganos. It has inch-long clusters of pale green bracts under which pink flowers peek. It is best displayed atop a wall so that these flowers can cascade over it. There are many other examples of excellent ornamentals waiting to be liberated from the herb garden. Herb gardens and nurseries are often treasure troves for the gardener searching for new ornamentals.

Ultimately what one does in his or her own garden has to meet only one criterion. It has to please the gardener. Whether one gathers all of one's herbs in a garden or allows them to mingle throughout the rest of the garden is a personal decision. But we have concluded that our herbs do not need their own garden for their successful cultivation and that they can add so much to the general garden with their beautiful flowers, leaves, forms and fragrances. 🦋

Mixed Border, Edible Border

Cynthia Gillis

The day of the separate kitchen garden is over for most of us. No longer is there a cutting garden out of sight behind a screen or hedge, tended by gardeners and used by cooks, leaving us to idle in beautifully designed, purely ornamental gardens.

Ocimum basilicum *'Spicy Globe' grows well in pots or in the garden border. The advantage to pot culture is that when the basil looks ragged from cutting, it can be moved out of sight.*

Today, most of us are our own cooks, our own gardeners, and in our small backyards we don't have space to hide the herbs we're going to harvest. The plants we grow for the kitchen also have to serve attractively in the garden.

Fortunately, many culinary herbs make utterly charming neighbors. They're attractive as plants, offering beautiful leaves or flowers and maintaining an attractive habit without a lot of propping up. They form

A mini-garden of herbs contains bay, 'Dark Opal' basil, chives, thyme, parsley and golden sage. Plants can be kept to size by frequent snipping.

Mint, blooming in the background, adds a fresh fragrance to the garden. It can be kept in bounds by using an underground barrier or by planting it in a pot and sinking the pot in the ground. A scented geranium adds an interesting texture to the foreground.

Cynthia Gillis gardens at her home in Brooklyn, New York. She is a garden designer whose writing has appeared in Horticulture *magazine.*

Photos by Elvin McDonald

pleasing combinations with other plants in the garden and accept the same cultural conditions as their companion plants. And they can be planted and combined so that when we snip away at them for the kitchen, the garden doesn't look any the worse for wear.

A plant that fully earns its keep this way is the nasturtium (*Tropaeolum majus*). A trailing or climbing annual, its large, round, blue-green leaves make a fast-growing ground cover and background filler-plant, showing off any other plants seen against it. Every year, I interplant some nasturtium seeds with a group of *Allium christophii* bulbs. The pale, silvery-mauve balls of allium flowers look better against the round nasturtium leaves than against their own leaves, and later, when the allium goes dormant, the nasturtium completely fills the space.

Nasturtium also combines well with lavender and lady's mantle (*Alchemilla mollis*). Together, the soft, gray-green needlelike leaves and shrubby habit of the lavender, the neatly pleated fan of leaves and curly-headed yellow-green flowers of the lady's mantle, and the profusion of the nasturtium make an enthralling trio of texture, color and growth habit.

As a kitchen plant, nasturtium is almost a one-plant band. The leaves are a peppery addition to salads (tasting much like watercress, whose botanical name, interestingly, is *Nasturtium officinale*). The buds and seeds can be pickled in vinegar and used as a substitute for capers. The sweetly fragrant flowers are often used as an edible garnish—lovely when floating on a cold summer soup.

The fresh fragrance of mint also makes it a welcome garden plant despite its inclination to take over the garden. The best way to control mint is to use an underground barrier or to plant mint in a pot and sink the pot into the ground. I once failed to heed the warnings about mint, and it spread throughout the flower bed, under the nearby stone patio, and eventually filled in all the spaces between the stones. Every time someone stepped onto my patio, the scent of mint was released.

For this reason I now deliberately grow mint this way, between paving stones, used the same way as thyme. It doesn't mind being stepped on, and when it is, the whole garden is filled with its fragrance. I cut it down to the ground when it appears where I don't want it.

One of my favorite late-summer dishes is an appetizer consisting of fresh figs halved lenghwise, a whole mint leaf placed on the cut side, and both wrapped in a strip of prosciutto ham with the green tip of the fresh mint leaf visible against the rosy ham.

I prefer to grow green basil (*Ocimum basilicum*) in containers. I don't find it particularly attractive in the garden until it flowers. And once it does flower its leaves become quite bitter and are no longer suitable for making pesto sauce, an uncooked basil-based sauce that's a staple of our summer menus.

My favorite recipe: Combine in a blender 2 packed cups of basil leaves, ½ cup olive oil, 2 tablespoons of pine nuts, 2 cloves of garlic. Blend these ingredients until they're smooth, then beat in by hand ½ cup fresh-grated parmesan and 2 tablespoons softened butter. Since a single recipe for this pesto sauce can use almost a whole basil plant (or large amounts cut from several plants), it can have a rather noticeable effect on the appearance of the garden. Containers with decimated basil plants can be moved out of sight to rejuvenate. I generally discard picked-over plants and replant with some other herb or flowering annual.

In the garden I find that purple basil (*Ocimum basilicum* 'Dark Opal') is a much more interesting ornamental plant. Purple basil makes an unexpected edging in front of *Rosa rubrifolia*, complementing its red-tinged, blue-green leaves and ruddy canes and also providing color after the roses' all-too-brief flowering period. *Sedum* 'Vera Jameson' also combines nicely with the basil and roses. Its blue-green, red-veined leaves and stems make it similar in overall color effect to the basil and the roses, and its thick, almost perfectly round succulent leaves provide textural contrast with the toothed, silky basil leaves. In the kitchen a few leaves of purple basil can be used as a colorful addition to a green salad, to season thick slices of ripe tomatoes or as an aromatic addition to stew.

One of the few herbs that grow in the shade is sweet woodruff (strictly *Asperula odorata* or *Galium odoratum*), the flavoring ingredient in May wine. To make this springtime punch, combine 12 sprigs of sweet woodruff, 1 cup of powdered sugar, 1 bottle of Moselle or other moderately dry German white wine. After about ½ hour, remove the sweet woodruff leaves, pour the mixture over a block of ice in a punch bowl, and add 1 quart of sparkling water. You can use fresh sprigs of sweet woodruff to decorate the punch.

Sweet woodruff makes a lovely ground cover in a shady, woodland area, and in the spring its tiny, white star-shaped flowers sparkle against the glossy whorls of its leaves. I've grown it in combination with drifts of *Lamium* 'White Nancy', whose white-variegated leaves and white flowers contrast elegantly with the sweet woodruff.

The first time I saw sweet cicely (*Myrrhis odorata*) I didn't know that it was an herb. I only knew I wanted it. It was planted in a mass, forming a graceful, feathery, three-foot-high hedge. A slight breeze was enough to release the sweet, anise fragrance that arises from every part of the plant. Adding some chopped cicely leaves to cooked, buttered carrots or sweet potatoes gives a light and interesting licorice aroma that complements the flavor of these sweet root vegetables.

Sweet cicely is another herb that will grow and flower in shade. Its clusters of white flowers (reminiscent of Queen Anne's Lace) and delicate foliage make it an attractive sight when planted in front of the deep green, coarse leaves of a rhododendron or leather-leaf viburnum (*Viburnum rhytidophyllum*).

Here are some other combinations of culinary herbs with ornamental plants that are visually pleasing:

Chives (*Allium schoenoprasum*) planted with a blue-flowering cranesbill geranium. The geranium gracefully flops over, so when I snip some chives for soup or a salad the geranium covers the spot. And since the chives flower before the geranium, that space in the garden is in flower for a very long time each summer.

Sage (*Salvia officinalis*) and rosemary (*Rosmarinus officinalis*) combine with lily-of-the-Nile (*Agapanthus africanus* 'Headbourne Hybrids') for a mostly edible summer flower border in blue and silver. The dark green, straplike leaves of lily-of-the Nile, and its tall, deep blue flowers make a dramatic contrast with the pale blue flower spikes and silver leaves of the sage and the soft-needled rosemary. And because the three plants grow into one another, I can use all the sage and rosemary I like, without damaging the visual effect.

This combination is beautiful year-round. In winter the soft, silver-green leaves of the sage take on a ruddy tone, creating a wonderful garden picture next to the shrubby evergreen rosemary.

If rosemary weren't hardy in my garden, I'd use a yew (*Taxus cuspidata*) in its place for a similar, fine-needled effect, keeping it pruned to about three feet. (Yew is an ornamental substitute, not a culinary one. It's extremely poisonous and has figured in many a murder mystery.) Similarly, *Allium giganteum* could substitute for the agapanthus.

My garden in Brooklyn, New York is in USDA Zone 7, where the average minimum temperature is about 0 to 10 degrees F. However the shelter provided by surrounding brownstone houses, and the use of deep winter mulch has helped me keep these tender plants thriving in the garden for four years.

The goal in a small space is to create a garden picture. Thus all the herbs that I grow, I would grow even if they had no culinary purpose. But fortunately, one doesn't have to choose, since so many beautiful plants are also so good to eat. ❧

Cooking with Less Common Herbs

Sal Gilbertie

Cress evokes childhood memories of picking the fresh green growth from the banks of a nearby creek and nibbling on the cold, peppery leaves. Whether it's grown wild on the banks of a stream or in the herb garden, you'll want plenty of cress for salads and superb cress soup. Of the several varieties of cress, watercress is the best known to the cook and most widely used. Garden cress is similar in flavor to watercress but slightly sharper and its leaves are smaller and a paler green.

Although not an aromatic herb, cress adds a peppery flavor (often described as a combination of the flavors of parsley, spinach and mustard greens) to everything from green or vegetable salads to pasta, fish, chicken, potatoes, soups and grains. Add minced cress leaves to hollandaise, béarnaise and beurre blanc. Add finely minced cress leaves to crepe batter, compound butters and crème fraîche (for topping grilled fish or chicken paillards). Include some minced cress in soufflés or fish mousse.

Chinese cooks use watercress for its pungent flavor in broth soups at the end of a rich meal and in stir-fry recipes with meat or chicken.

Cress is the traditional English sandwich stuffer or topping on finger sandwiches for the tea table. Mix fresh cress with radish, alfalfa and bean sprouts for a crunchy filling for sandwiches or crepes—or toss with a mustard vinaigrette for a salad rich in texture and flavor.

For an elegant first course, arrange rolled slices of lightly smoked salmon on a bed of watercress. Add slices of hard-cooked egg and offer a dill vinaigrette. Sprinkle on capers; add a few nasturtium blossoms for a beautiful presentation.

If you grow arugula (roquette) in your garden, combine equal amounts of finely chopped watercress and arugula with grated onion, a dash of Tabasco, a squeeze of lemon and just enough sour cream to bind. Offer the spread in a pretty bowl, surrounded with toast points.

Foeniculum vulgare dulce, *Florence fennel, is an essential kitchen herb. The bulb and tender stems have been a familiar vegetable for quite some time, but an increasing number of cooks are using the feathery foliage in their recipes.*

Sal Gilbertie runs Gilbertie's Herb Farm, a family business which has become one of the foremost herb nurseries in the country. Kitchen Herbs: The Art and Enjoyment of Growing Herbs and Cooking with Them *is his first book.*

Watercress, which grows wild on stream banks, can be grown in a pot partially submerged in water. This herb is a superb addition to salads and soups. Its peppery flavor adds to almost any dish.

Add some sprightly sprigs of cress to gazpacho. Tuck the tender stems into pita bread filled with rare roast beef. Top with a dollop of sour cream and the best caviar that you can afford for a peasant sandwich worthy of a special occasion.

For a refreshing and healthful drink, throw some watercress in a blender with cold tomato juice, some fresh basil leaves and a dash of Tabasco. Chopped cress is excellent mixed with mayonnaise as a salad dressing. Add the leaves to potato salad, chicken salad or seafood salad, just before serving.

Cress is best eaten raw or cooked briefly. It will not dry or freeze. To keep cress fresh once picked, store it in the refrigerator with the stems in water and the leaves covered by a plastic bag. Plan to use the cress within a day or two.

Excerpted from *Kitchen Herbs: The Art and Enjoyment of Growing Herbs and Cooking with Them*, Bantam Books, NY 1988

Lady Apple and Blue Cheese Salad with Pomegranate Dressing

Serves 4

Rich with autumn colors, this spectacular salad has a combination of flavors that makes it perfect for a roast chicken or duck dinner. The tart, stylish dressing is especially good with fresh watercress.

12 lady apples*
Fresh lemon juice
4 cups watercress leaves and tender stems
¼ pound blue cheese, crumbled
⅓ cup olive oil
3 tablespoons raspberry vinegar
1 shallot, minced
¼ cup pomegranate seeds from
  1 pomegranate**
Salt and freshly ground black pepper to
  taste

Cut apples in half lengthwise; stem and core. Rub cut surfaces with lemon juice. Wash and thoroughly dry watercress. Tear watercress into bite-size pieces and divide equally among 4 chilled salad plates or shallow bowls.

Arrange 6 apple halves on each plate; sprinkle with blue cheese. Whisk together oil, vinegar and shallot. Stir in pomegranate seeds. Sprinkle salads with salt and pepper to taste. Spoon on dressing.

Lady apples are very small white apples with a red blush that are available from mid-October through December. If not available, substitute wedges of red or yellow Delicious apples or seckel pears.
**To remove the seeds, cut the pomegranate in quarters and remove the flesh from the shell with a spoon. Remove and discard the connecting pulp.*

Cooking with Fennel

For Italian and French cooks, fennel is an essential kitchen herb. Its delicate anise flavor is valued for fish, sausages, salads, breads and pasta. For years, the bulb and tender young stems of Florence fennel (also called finocchio) have been a familiar vegetable in American kitchens but increasingly the herb fennel is becoming popular—its leaves and seeds are also used with poultry, pork, soups and cooked vegetables such as cabbage, peas, beans, potatoes and cauliflower. All parts of this graceful Mediterranean plant can be used in cooking.

The feathery green leaves are wonderful with fish. Stuff whole fish with the leaves and stalks before roasting or grilling. Add the leaves to a poaching liquid or to a basting sauce. For a quick fish butter, combine ¼ cup (½ stick) unsalted butter, 2 teaspoons lemon juice, salt and freshly ground black pepper to taste, 2 tablespoons finely chopped fennel leaves and a dash of Pernod.

Stir the chopped leaves into hot tomato soup to heighten its flavor, add them to meat loaves and polenta. Sprinkle them over salads or into marinades. Chopped fresh fennel does wonders for white bean salad.

Add the crushed fennel seeds to crumb toppings for casseroles, press them into pork chops before grilling or stir them into bread dough, steamed cabbage or a spicy sausage sauce for pasta. Use fennel seed in combination with the chopped fresh leaves as an aromatic stuffing poked into slits cut in a pork roast.

Treat the hollow stalks as you would celery in cooking. Eat them raw or simmer the stalks in water or chicken stock as a vegetable to be served with butter. They can also be sautéed in garlic and olive oil. Add them to soups or stews (at the last as they cook quickly). Children love the licoricelike flavor of fennel; let them use a fresh fennel stalk as a straw for sipping orange juice. In the South of France, the dried fennel stalks are the bed on which grilled sea bass is flamed. Try adding a few sprigs of fresh rosemary to the fennel for a fantastic flavor and aroma.

The root can be thinly sliced and simmered in chicken stock until tender for a simple fennel soup, adding salt and freshly ground black pepper to taste. The clusters of lovely yellow flowers in late summer and early fall are beautiful as a garnish.

Make fennel vinegar and then use the vinegar for *buerre blanc* fennel sauce. The leaves can be dried but they will lose some of their pungency. Fresh fennel leaves can be frozen for up to two months, packed in small bunches in plastic bags. Use them as you would fresh.

Flamed Tuna with Fennel and Tangerine Sauce

Serves 4

This is a variation of the famous French method of flaming fish with fennel using fresh tuna, which is deliciously meaty when cooked in this manner. Serve wild rice and a julienne of zucchini and carrots with the fish.

4 thick tuna steaks (about 6 ounces each)
Salt and freshly ground black pepper to taste
¼ cup olive oil
2 tbls. chopped fresh fennel leaves
2 tbls. chopped flat-leaf parsley
Dried fennel stalks
Cognac for flaming, warmed
Fresh fennel sprigs, tarragon sprigs and edible flowers for garnish

Grated zest of 2 tangerines
Tangerine sauce (recipe follows)

Sprinkle tuna with salt and pepper, to taste. In a small bowl, combine olive oil, fennel and parsley. Grill tuna over hot coals about 3 to 4 minutes per side, until brown on the outside but slightly pink inside, basting with fennel oil.

Arrange fish over dried fennel stalks on a flameproof platter. Pour over warm Cognac and flame. Spoon sauce onto individual serving plates. Arrange tuna over sauce and garnish with herbs and edible flowers. Sprinkle with tangerine zest. Serve with remaining Tangerine sauce.

Tangerine sauce:

½ cup fresh tangerine juice
2 tsp. chopped fresh tarragon
¼ cup unsalted butter, cut into 4 pieces

Bring tangerine juice and tarragon to a boil in a small saucepan. Whisk in ¼ cup butter, piece by piece, until sauce thickens.

Cooking with Sorrel

For those who love sorrel, it's the star of the kitchen herb garden in the spring, evoking childhood memories of nibbling on sour grass. Sorrel is much like garlic, either loved with a passion or disdained with an equal passion. A staple in the French kitchen, sorrel tastes like sharp, sprightly spinach with a sour, lemony tang.

Sorrel can be overwhelming until you've acquired a taste for its sharp flavor; add it slowly, tasting as you go. A bit of chopped sorrel will hide the fact that you've omitted salt.

Keep a chiffonade of fresh sorrel, cooked in a skillet with a little unsalted butter until it literally melts, in the refrigerator to blend into soups, sauces, dips and dressings; for filling an omelet; and for topping a baked potato or poached fish. Serve poached eggs on a bed of sorrel chiffonade that has been wilted with finely minced shallots for a summer brunch.

When whole large sorrel leaves are used as a wrapping for cooking, they impart a tenderizing effect as well as lending their subtle tartness for flavoring. Wrap jumbo sea scallops in large sorrel leaves. Steam-cook for 3 to 4 minutes and serve with a lime butter sauce. Use the tender leaves in place of lettuce in hot or cold sandwiches and hamburgers. Offer finely shredded sorrel for tacos and tostadas.

Tear the young leaves for salads of greens, cabbage or potatoes, discarding the stems and center ribs of larger leaves. When using sorrel for a green or cabbage salad, wrap the washed leaves in paper towels and store in refrigerator to crisp before adding. Cut back somewhat on the vinegar or lemon juice in the dressing. Shred fresh sorrel into radicchio leaves. Top with sliced fresh mushrooms and chopped fresh tomato that have been warmed in a little olive oil. Sprinkle lightly with red wine vinegar. Add salt and freshly ground black pepper to taste.

Stir chopped fresh sorrel into your favorite gazpacho before chilling. Add shredded sorrel to a fish soup. Stir chopped sorrel into a beurre blanc to spoon over broiled salmon fillets. Additional fresh sorrel as a garnish will reinforce the clean flavor.

Try spinach and sorrel together for a subtle, flavorful combination. Add sorrel to creamed spinach, a spinach soufflé or spinach soup or just wilt sorrel and spinach together and toss with unsalted butter and a few grains of grated nutmeg.

Sorrel is widely used in Russia; it's virtually unused in England, Italy and other Mediterranean countries. The French use sorrel primarily in two ways: in soups and sauces.

Their sorrel soup is a world classic, loved for its delicate sour taste. The soup is served hot or cold, enriched with a spoonful of crème fraiche or sour cream and chopped fresh sorrel.

To keep the bright green color of sorrel, quick cooking is essential. Heat will cause the color to fade quickly, so add sorrel at the last minute.

Sorrel does not dry well. If your herb garden is prolific, you can freeze sorrel by puréeing the leaves; pack into freezer containers for a taste of summer during the dead of winter. Stir the purée into soups or mayonnaise to use as a sauce for poached fish or as a spread for sandwiches.

Scallop Salad with Sorrel Dressing

Serves 4

Ideal for salads, the tender leaves of raw sorrel impart their natural tartness to poached sea scallops in this colorful salad. The tangy, sour leaves are also in the dressing. Serve with crusty rolls and glasses of white wine for a casual summer luncheon on the patio.

1 pound sea scallops
½ cup dry white wine
½ cup water
2 shallots, finely minced
3 cups loosely packed small sorrel leaves
2 tbls. white wine vinegar
2 tsp. dry mustard
1 tsp. sugar
½ cup olive oil
2 ripe avocados
2 large sweet red peppers, peeled and sliced in thin julienne strips
2 tbls. chopped fresh chervil

Rinse scallops. In a large heavy skillet, combine wine, water and shallots; bring to a boil. Add scallops; cover and poach for 5 minutes, or until scallops are just opaque in center when cut. Drain and chill until cold.

Rinse sorrel; trim off and discard any coarse stems. Chop enough leaves to make 2 tablespoons. Set aside. Wrap remaining sorrel leaves in paper towels, enclose in a plastic bag and chill in the refrigerator to crisp.

In a food processor or blender, combine reserved 2 tablespoons chopped sorrel leaves, vinegar, dry mustard and sugar. Process until mixture is a purée. With motor running, slowly add oil through the feed tube and process until well blended.

To assemble salads, place the sorrel on 4 chilled serving plates. Peel, pit and slice avocados; fan out on the greens. Arrange the scallops and red peppers on plates. Drizzle each salad with prepared sorrel dressing and garnish with chopped chervil.

Cooking with Lovage

Lovage is an old-fashioned herb with a distinctive flavor—like pungent celery with a hint of lemon and anise. If you've never eaten lovage, use it cautiously at first. Cut the leaves or tender stalks for soups and use a few chopped sprigs in salads. A little lovage goes a long way.

All parts of this magnificent Mediterranean herb are used in cooking. Use the leaves as you would any other aromatic herb in salads, stuffings, vegetable soups and omelets. Cut and blanch the young hollow stalks as a vegetable, chop them into soups and sauces or candy them as you would angelica for garnishing cakes. Use tougher mature stalks in chicken or beef stock.

Fill the cavity of a nonoily fish such as red snapper or trout with lovage stems and leaves. Baste with olive oil infused with chopped lovage leaves while grilling or baking. Flame with a splash of Pernod.

When cooked, fresh lovage is not as pungent in flavor. Lovage seeds dry well; sprinkle them over meat or into bread dough. Lovage seeds also make a flavorful herb butter. Grate the lovage roots to make tea or chop them and preserve in honey for basting ham and pork.

A preservation method that works well with lovage is the salt method; sprinkle ½ teaspoon salt per 1 cup of loosely packed chopped lovage. Alternate ½-inch-thick layers of chopped lovage with salt sprinklings until the container is full. Refrigerate. Use this lovage salt instead of table salt for cooking.

Lovage Frittata

Serves 4

Lovage and frittatas—huge thick omelets baked in the oven—are both native to the Mediterranean. Perfect for brunch, lunch or supper, frittatas are wonderfully flexible and can be quickly made with whatever vegetables and herbs you have on hand. For a light Sunday lunch, serve this frittata with hot, crusty herb bread and an arugula (roquette) and garden lettuce salad. Offer iced cherries or champagne grapes and your best homemade cookies for dessert.

3 tbls. olive oil
2 medium baking potatoes, peeled and
*   thinly sliced*
1 medium onion, peeled and thinly sliced
½ cup loosely packed lovage leaves
2 sweet red peppers, minced
8 eggs, lightly beaten

Many soups benefit from the addition of herbs. Pictured here is a cold, creamy avocado soup garnished with cilantro.

Salt and freshly ground black pepper to
*   taste*
2 sprigs of fresh thyme

Preheat oven to 400°.

Pour the olive oil into an 8-inch baking dish.

Arrange potato and onion sliced in the baking dish; bake for 20 minutes, or until potatoes are just tender. Sprinkle lovage and red peppers over the other vegetables. Pour eggs over vegetables and sprinkle with salt and pepper to taste. Arrange thyme on top.

Bake until eggs are set, the sides are puffed and the top is golden brown, about 20 minutes. The frittata should be firm but not dry. Serve hot or at room temperature.

Strasbourg Hens with Lovage Stuffing

Serves 2

Fresh lovage adds the perfect flavor accent to the stuffing for these game hens served with a beer sauce. Finish this country meal with

two fresh vegetable purées, beet and carrot. For dessert, make a rhubarb crisp served with spoonfuls of crème fraîche.

1 small onion, minced
1 carrot, finely diced
⅓ cup finely chopped fresh lovage (use the tender young shoots and leaves)
2 tbls. salted butter
1 bay leaf
1 sprig of fresh thyme
½ cup wild rice
2½ cups chicken stock (preferably homemade)
Salt and freshly ground black pepper to taste
2 ¾-pound Cornish hens
2 slices bacon
1½ cups light beer, at room temperature
½ tsp. sugar
1 carrot, peeled and cut in fine julienne strips
1 leek (white part only), washed and cut in fine julienne strips
Salt and freshly ground black pepper to taste

To make stuffing, sauté onion, carrot and lovage in butter for 10 minutes. Add bay leaf, thyme and wild rice. Add 1 cup chicken stock. Bring to a boil; cover and reduce heat to low. Cook for about 30 minutes, stirring occasionally with a fork to prevent sticking. Add salt and pepper to taste. When rice is tender, remove thyme sprig, drain off any excess liquid and set stuffing aside to cool slightly.

Preheat oven to 350°.

While stuffing is cooling, debone hens by turning the hen breast side down on a cutting board. With a sharp knife, cut down both sides of the backbone. Remove meat from the rib cage, cutting as close to the bone as possible. Cut away the whole carcass from the meat. Remove the thigh bones from each leg and turn the hen skin side up. (If you're on good terms with your butcher, ask him to debone the hens for you.)

Carefully loosen the skin from the meat. Insert ½ cup of prepared stuffing under the skin of each hen. Turn hen over and fasten skin closed with a small skewer. Tuck wing tips under breast and tie the drumsticks together with kitchen string. Place hens breast side up in a shallow baking dish.

Cut bacon slices in half and cover each hen with two strips. Roast for about 45 minutes, until golden brown. Remove hens from pan, remove skewers and keep warm. Drain off the excess grease from the roasting pan; add ½ cup beer to deglaze. Strain into a saucepan; add remaining 1½ cups chicken stock and set aside.

In a large heavy skillet, combine remaining 1 cup beer and sugar. Bring to a boil over medium-high heat. Add the carrot and leek. Cook about 3 minutes or until just tender. Lift out the cooked vegetables and keep warm. Add the vegetable juices to the reserved pan juices and reduce over high heat to thicken. Add salt and pepper to taste.

Remove bacon from the roasted hens. Place on individual heated serving plates and garnish with julienne vegetables. Nap hens and vegetables with the reduced sauce. ◢

Lavender   Lavandula angustifolia

Hardy Herbs for Northern Gardens

Roy Barrette

In England the word herb is pronounced herb, in America usually urb. *The American Heritage Dictionary* gives urb as the preferred pronunciation. *The Oxford English Dictionary* prefers herb but gives erbe as Middle English and says the H was added in the 19th century. The Americans were, apparently, well satisfied with urb or erbe and stuck with it. In any event both dictionaries agree that a herb, or an erbe, take your choice, is a plant that has (1) a fleshy stem that dies to the ground in the winter or (2) is used especially for medicine, scent or flavoring. Most people in both countries think of herbs as falling into the latter category.

While almost all gardens have some plants falling into classification (2) there are enthusiasts, such as members of The American Herb Society, who have whole gardens or parts of them especially set aside for plants that are fragrant, flavorful or medicinal. These are what people think of as herb gardens. I do not have an herb garden as such, but I cultivate about two acres of shrubs and perennials, and a few annuals, which include plants falling into the popular understanding of what constitutes an herb. I think most gardeners do.

I live on the coast of Maine and am fortunate in being within 800 feet of the lower reaches of a large bay so that the ameliorating effects of the salt water (if it is not frozen) places my garden in Zone 5/6; a few miles inland it is 10 degrees colder in the winter and much hotter during the summer. I mention this as an important factor in growing all plants, as well as microclimates—north or south of a wall, a boulder or a building.

My favorite herb is rosemary—Shakespeare's plant for remembrance. I have four bushes which are planted every spring at the feet of a couple of espaliered pears. Every summer some delighted visitor says "I didn't know you could grow rosemary in Maine." You can't, outdoors, but I dig mine every fall after frost, cutting back roots and top fiercely and stuffing them into 12-inch pots that are taken into the cold end (45 degree night temperature) of my greenhouse where they rest all winter. In the spring they are planted out and by fall are over three-feet tall. They propagate easily from four-inch summer cuttings. I have enjoyed my old plants for 20 years. They are tolerant of neglect. *The Royal Horticultural Society Dictionary of Gardening* says that Marian Cran, whose name is familiar to most gardeners, recommends a mixture of rosemary, mint, tansy and thyme plus some ground cloves as a moth destroyer. I've never tried it so can't confirm that it repels moths, but I'll bet it smells good.

Another of my friends among the herbs is lavender. It is hardier than rosemary but in this climate is a sometime thing. I have two large plants outside the south end of my greenhouse that have been happy for 15 years. They were given to me by a woman who lives high up in the Berkshire hills; she grew them from

Roy Barrette's column, "The Retir'd Gardener," ran in The Ellsworth American *for 23 years. In July 1989, when Barrette celebrated his 92nd birthday, the retired gardener became the tired gardener, and the column ceased. His writings have been published in* Yankee *magazine and several newspapers, and his garden at Amen Farm in Brooklin, Maine, was profiled in* Horticulture *magazine in 1987.*

Photo by Elvin McDonald

Tarragon ready for the addition of vinegar. The French variety is much more flavorful than the Russian.

Tarragon has been gathered in preparation for making vinegar. Herbal vinegars are easy to make and much less expensive than the ones in gourmet shops.

seed, but 16 of their clones grown from cuttings died last winter. They were five years old, grown as a hedge and had a western exposure. I now have 50 year-old plants under cloche and fir mulch in my kitchen garden. They are said to be 'Munstead Dwarf'. I await the spring with interest and a little apprehension.

In my garden chives provide an edging to a flower bed. The row is about 30 feet long. We cut it early in the year before blossoming and put what we need in the freezer. As thrift (*Armeria*) of old fashioned gardens is not quite hardy with us, we use chives (*Allium schoenoprasum*) in its place. It is rather more buxom but serves well enough as a substitute. I also grow what are known as garlic chives, which have flat leaves and are much more delicate in appearance, as clumps in my flower border. The leaves have a faint smell of garlic and are wonderful in a green salad but their flowers are delightfully fragrant. I pot up a few clumps in the fall and leave them out until the tops die down and then bring them into the greenhouse for early spring forcing.

Here is an array of vinegars prepared from many different herbs. Not only are these vinegars flavorful, but they are attractive as well, especially with the light shining through them. They make excellent gifts.

Tarragon (*Artemisia dracunculus*) grows well in a southern exposure. In midsummer we use the leaves in fish recipes and also to make tarragon vinegar. You can make enough tarragon vinegar to float a battleship from a couple of bushes and it won't cost you as much as a fancy bottle that only holds about a half pint from the supermarket. When you buy your plants be sure you get the French variety with smooth, dark green leaves. It is much more flavorful than Russian.

I don't know if sorrel (*Rumex scutatus*) is considered an herb that falls in category (2), but we think it flavorful and grow it to make sorrel soup. It is an easy perennial, and one can pick from a few plants all summer. *JOY OF COOKING* has a tasty recipe for cream of sorrel soup. Sorrel, whose leaves resemble those of dock, belongs to the same family and is about as hard to kill once it gets hold, so plant it where you expect to leave it. Generally, herbs are tough, tenacious plants; give them reasonably good treatment and they will last for years. 🌿

New Ways with Herbs

Recipes From Le Gourmand

Bruce Naftaly & Robin Sanders

At Le Gourmand we get to enjoy ourselves improvising with flavors and textures of the wonderful variety of ingredients available to us in the Northwest. Over the years we have developed a network of suppliers—small orange farmers, fishermen, mushroom gatherers—who provide us with the materials with which we work.

Fresh herbs have always played an important part in our cooking. We use them in three basic ways: first, simply as distinct flavorings in themselves such as basil with tomatoes, garlic and olive oil over fresh goat cheese, or in a sauce for the albacore tuna which runs off the Washington and Oregon coasts in August—just in time for the tomatoes and basil. Or maybe French tarragon for a simple roast chicken or in a rich butter sauce for our crayfish. Or sorrel for our rich, tangy sorrel soup.

An early spring menu features a lamb stew containing many herbs and vegetables accompanied by a salad of greens including arugula with a hot bacon dressing. A crusty bread completes the menu.

Photo by Inger Skaarup

Photo by Elvin McDonald

A bouquet of different basils complements the tray of cheeses and other hors d'oeuvres about to be served.

Secondly, we use fresh herbs for their ability in certain combinations to enhance the flavor of something—perhaps you won't taste the herb itself, but whatever you are eating will taste better than anything you have ever eaten. My favorite example is the magic that fresh lovage does to mussels.

Lastly, we combine herbs and other ingredients, such as fruits, with rich stocks to produce complex sauces. In this situation the flavors combine to create a new flavor with its own individual character. Apple and tarragon do this, as do apple and sage. Peaches and basil, and gooseberries with dill, are also favorite combinations and are featured in the recipes that follow.

There are no "right" or "wrong" combinations or uses for herbs. As with so many things, what one finds delicious is literally a question of taste. The recipes that follow are products of much experimentation. We encourage others to have fun. Experiment, improvise. Think of the menu—what you'd like to taste with what. The garden is the limit.

Mussels Steamed with White Wine and Fresh Lovage

2 lbs. fresh mussels (Washington State preferred)
1 cup dry white wine
½ cup fresh lovage leaves
¼ lb. melted, unsalted butter

Beard mussels. In a non-aluminum pan add wine, lovage and mussels. Cover and steam until mussels are open. Transfer to a large serving platter or individual bowls. Generously ladle steaming liquid and melted butter over the cooked mussels and serve garnished with fresh lovage leaves and accompanied with lots of sourdough bread. Here, lovage is used to complement and intensify the sweet and rich taste of the mussels.

Fresh basil combines with ripe peaches to create an intriguing and spicy flavor that perfectly complements the slightly gamey, complex, rich, but not heavy taste of the rabbit. This dish is also good cold.

Sautéed Rabbit with Peach and Basil Sauce

2 cut-up rabbit fryers

Sauce
4 medium-sized ripe peaches—peeled, pitted and cut into small pieces
3 cups rich, dark brown rabbit or veal stock
¾ cup fresh basil leaves, coarsely chopped
3 tbls. cognac
salt, freshly ground white pepper

2 medium-sized ripe, fresh peaches, peeled and cut into wedges for garnish

Sauté the rabbits: Brown pieces on all sides in hot oil. Add a small amount (about 1 tbls.) stock to pan and reduce heat to low and cover and cook for about 20 minutes. When done, remove rabbit pieces to hot serving platter (or individual plates) and reduce liquid in pan to 2 tbls. and add to sauce. Finish seasoning the

sauce and serve over the rabbit. Garnish with fresh basil leaves and the peach wedges that have been gently poached in the sauce for 5 minutes.

Sauce
Simmer peaches and stock in non-aluminum saucepan 45 minutes until peaches are soft and stock is reduced to 2 cups. Transfer to food processor and purée. Return to saucepan and simmer, skimming occasionally for another 15 minutes. Add chopped basil and cognac and simmer for 10 minutes. Season to taste with salt and freshly ground white pepper—it will take more salt than you think. Correct texture by either reducing slightly or by adding more stock. Just before serving, poach the peach garnishes in the sauce for 5 minutes.

Our own improvisation on an old French dish of a sauce made of late spring's tart gooseberries with rich, oily mackerel. Here, the gooseberries are combined with fresh dill and reduced fish stock and served with our lovely king salmon. As in the old recipe, the tart gooseberries are a perfect foil for the rich salmon. However, the addition of fresh dill and reduced fish stock to the sauce produce a wonderful, balanced, focused flavor that enhances the salmon and is truly delicious. One of my favorites!

Poached King Salmon Fillet with Gooseberry and Dill Sauce

4 8-oz fresh king salmon fillets

½ pint fresh gooseberries (top and tail ¼ cup of the berries and save for garnish)
*4 cups white wine fish stock
½ cup whipping cream
¼ cup fresh dill
Salt, freshly ground white pepper

Sauce
In a non-aluminum saucepan gently simmer the gooseberries with 2 tbls. of the stock until berries are soft. Purée in food mill or food processor and strain through a fine strainer to eliminate stems and skins. Set aside. In a

non-aluminum saucepan, reduce the fish stock to 3 tbls. (!). Add whipping cream and reduce by ⅔. Add gooseberry purée and dill and bring to simmer. Season with salt and freshly ground white pepper. Correct texture with either more stock or cream, or reduce further. Add topped and tailed gooseberries 5 minutes to gently poach before serving.

*recipe follows

Salmon

Poach salmon fillets in a simple court bouillon (½ leek white, parsley, thyme) until just done—about 10 minutes. Drain and blot the fillets fairly dry in order to avoid diluting the sauce with the poaching liquid from the fish. Serve immediately with the above sauce.

White Wine Fish Stock

4 lbs. white fish bones (halibut is best) rinsed in cold water and cut into small pieces
1 medium onion, coarsely chopped
1 medium leek, coarsely chopped
4 cups dry white wine

In a non-aluminum saucepan, steam the leeks and onions in one half of the wine, covered, until they become translucent and "relax"—about 10 minutes. Add the fish bones and the rest of the wine, cover and steam an additional 10 minutes. Add enough cold water to cover the ingredients. Bring to a boil and simmer, skimming, for 25 minutes. Strain through the finest strainer and/or cheesecloth.

Fresh sage combines with apples to produce a rich, mellow, deep flavor of its own which captures the essence of autumn when combined with the roast pheasant.

Roast Pheasant with Apple and Sage Sauce

2 3½–lb. pheasants, halved
*3 cups dark brown pheasant (or poultry) stock

2 cups coarsely chopped, peeled and cored apples (your favorite sauce apple)
3 tbls. chopped fresh sage
¾ cup whipping cream
¼ cup calvados
salt and freshly ground black pepper
2 tbls. unsalted butter

Garnish

1½ medium apples peeled, cored and thinly sliced
sage leaves

*recipe follows

Sauce

Bring stock to simmer in a heavy medium-sized non-aluminum saucepan. Add apple pieces and chopped sage and simmer over low heat until apples are tender and liquid has reduced by half, skimming surface—about one hour. Transfer to food processor and purée. Sieve through fine strainer into heavy small saucepan, add cream and boil until reduced to saucelike consistency.

Birds

Using sharp knife separate pheasant breast from rib cage (save rib cage for stock!). Leave breasts, thighs, legs and wings intact. Brown all sides in hot oil in roasting pan and roast in hot oven (475°) breast side up about 15 minutes, until juices run pale pink when thigh is pierced. Transfer pheasant to serving platter. Pour off fat from pan. Set pan over high heat, deglaze with 1 tbls. calvados, scraping up browned bits. Add to sauce and rewarm sauce. Season with salt and pepper.

Meanwhile, melt butter in heavy large skillet over medium heat. Add apple slices and cook until just tender and golden brown—about 5 minutes. Add remaining calvados and boil until reduced to a glaze. Spoon sauce onto plates. Top with pheasant. Garnish with sautéed apples and sage leaves.

*Dark Brown Stock

4 lbs. bones (veal, pheasant, chicken, etc.) cut into small pieces
4 celery stalks, coarsely chopped

1 large onion, coarsely chopped
2 medium carrots, coarsely chopped
small bunches of: thyme, sweet marjoram,
    rosemary, parsley, bay leaves
2 cups dry red wine

Brown bones in hot oil in large heavy-bottomed non-aluminum stockpot. Brown and scrape bones—about 20 minutes. Add veggies and continue browning and scraping 15 minutes, deglaze pan with red wine. Scrape up browned bits from pan bottom. Reduce wine by ⅔. Add enough cold water to just cover ingredients. Simmer slowly and skim surface for about 10 hours. Strain. Degrease.

This basket contains a charming collection of fresh herbs, including parsley, basil and garlic chives.

Repeat steps above with fresh ingredients! Add to the first stock. Then repeat a third and final time to make a "third stock"—rich, intensely flavored and dark brown.

Rillettes of Salmon

½ lb. smoked salmon
2 oz. fresh salmon fillet
2 oz. crème fraîche
¼ cup chopped chervil

⅛ cup chopped sweet cicely
½ small leek, parsley sprig, thyme branch

Poach the salmon fillet in a little court bouillon made with the leek, parsley and thyme—about 5 minutes, until just done. Remove salmon from bouillon and refrigerate to cool. Finely chop the chervil and sweet cicely and put in a mixing bowl. Put smoked salmon and cooled cooked salmon fillet in food processor and shred coarsely. Add to herbs in mixing bowl. Add crème fraîche and mix. Mold. Chill. Serve with homemade crackers or sourdough bread.

Homemade Mustard

1 quart water
½ cup yellow mustard seeds
¼ cup fresh sweet marjoram leaves
⅛ cup fresh summer savory leaves
5 tbls. extra virgin olive oil
3 tbls. intensely flavored 25-year-old sherry
    vinegar (or other intensely flavored
    vinegar)
1 tbls. manzanilla sherry (or verjus)
¼ tsp. salt

Combine water and mustard seeds in saucepan and bring to boil. Reduce heat and simmer for 15 minutes stirring occasionally. Drain seeds, rinse under cold water to cool —being careful not to rinse off all of the mustard oil that coats the seeds. Transfer seeds to food processor and purée to paste. Add remaining ingredients and blend well—mixture will not be smooth. Transfer to jar and refrigerate. Prepare a few days in advance of serving as flavor improves over time.

We love mustard and think everyone should make it! It is as easy as vinaigrette and provides an excellent opportunity to play with flavor combinations. Think of what the mustard will accompany and imagine. . . .We use the mustard in dressings, marinades, mayonnaises. It is a good background for many sauces. Improves with age in the refrigerator.✍

Herbs for Short Season, Cold Winter Areas

Diane Bilderback

Herbal breads fragrant with basil, thyme and oregano, lasagna flavored with basil or barbequed chicken spiced with oregano make my family especially appreciative of the herbs grown in our garden here in western Montana. We grow most of our own vegetables and freeze the excess for winter eating; a plentiful supply of dried or frozen herbs adds the much needed spice to our meals during our long winters.

Some winters are mild, while others have temperatures as low as −30 to −35 °F. By early December, we often have a foot of snow, which helps protect most of the perennial herbs. (Frequent thaws melt the snow cover, but generally snow is present when we need it to protect our plants from extremely low temperatures.) Springs are often cold and cloudy, postponing the last frost to the first week of June. Once June, our wettest month, is over, summertime temperatures soar into the 90s during the day, yet can fall into the 40s at night. There is generally little summer rain, making weekly irrigation necessary. The first fall frosts generally come within the first week of September, making our growing season often only 90 days long. Despite the climate, it is easy to grow an abundant supply of great tasting herbs.

Tender herbs that won't survive winter temperatures of −20 °F and below, or annuals that need to be replanted every year, include all basil varieties, rosemary, chervil, fennel, sweet marjoram and summer savory.

Diane Bilderback has been gardening in Missoula, Montana, since 1973. She has written many articles for Organic Gardening *magazine,* National Gardening *and* Family Circle. *Her books, written collaboratively with Dorothy Patent, include* Garden Secrets *and* Backyard Fruits and Berries.

Photo by Elvin McDonald

The author, who uses copious amounts of basil in tomato sauces, grows 30 to 40 plants of 'Spicy Globe', pictured here. Plant 'Spicy Globe' with other basils such as 'Dark Opal' and sweet basil in the border.

These varieties (except rosemary) can be seeded indoors six to eight weeks before planting in the garden after the last spring frost. Rosemary is generally started from cuttings. We plant it out in the garden during summer, then in the fall, dig and place it in our west-facing window for the winter. We use large amounts of basil in our tomato sauces and so grow 30 to 40 plants of 'Spicy Globe' basil. These can be planted with other basil varieties or as a border around other herbs or vegetables because of their unique six-to-eight-inch globe shape. I've also found that this variety can withstand low winter light conditions and does very well when planted in early January and placed in our west-facing window. In March, I transfer the potted plants to a frost-free cold frame and harvest throughout the early spring. Basil is available in wonderful shades of green, red and purple as well as small, medium and very large leaf forms. I like to group them together in the garden. Taller, large-leaved forms such as lettuce-leaf basil or 'Green Ruffles' go in the center, surrounded with smaller-leaved varieties such as lemon basil or piccolo basil. The outer perimeter of the block is outlined with 'Spicy Globe' basil. Spaced about six inches apart, the herbs make solid, colorful blocks. For the fastest growth and best-tasting leaves, plant these herbs in rich, well-drained soil in full sun. Our pH is slightly alkaline (-7.0), but the herbs don't seem to mind. During the last of a hot July and August, I often place a light, two- to three-inch mulch of grass clippings around the plants.

While I do dry these herbs for storage, I also mince large amounts of basil (I use a food processor), freeze it in a ice cube tray and then store the cubes in a plastic bag. While most recipes for freezing tell you to add oil before freezing, I have had good luck freezing the minced leaves alone. These cubes are just the right size to add to lasagna or other Italian sauces, soups or vegetables as they are cooking, and the flavor is closer to fresh than dried basil. For pesto, I defrost four cubes and add ¼ cup parmesan cheese, ½ tsp. salt and 1 finely minced garlic clove and mix well. This mixture is then stirred into 2 cups of hot pasta. While it is traditional to include some olive oil and pine nuts in pesto, we have chosen to leave these items out in an effort to lessen the fat content of the dish.

Some herbs which once planted and allowed to go to seed often magically reappear each spring: these include parsley, coriander (also known as cilantro), dill, arugula or roquette, borage and chamomile. Leave the seedlings where they come up or move them soon after germination to a more appropriate spot. Parsley has been a favorite herb ever since the birth of my second son Chris, who for the first five years of his life wouldn't eat anything green except parsley. We also use large amounts of it in tomato sauce. I grow parsley on my winter windowsill and have found that the curled varieties do better than the flat-leaf varieties under low-light conditions. In the early spring, as soon as the ground can be worked, I plant rows of curled varieties such as 'Forest Green', which has stiff upright stems, and Italian flat-leaf parsley that has a stronger flavor. I also plant smaller rows of cilantro, and the seedlings that appear aren't enough to satisfy our appetite for this herb. Dill, arugula, borage and chamomile reseed themselves so well that I never have to reseed.

Perennial herbs that grow without special winter care include spearmint, peppermint, sage varieties, thyme varieties, true oregano, true French tarragon, lavender, regular and Chinese or garlic chives and sorrel. We love sorrel so much that we have planted a three-foot by two-foot bed which in early spring we cover with a light cold frame. This encourages quick growth and early spring harvests. All these herbs except thyme varieties and French tarragon need full sun to grow quickly and yield abundantly. French tarragon and thyme can tolerate shade for part of the day and still yield well. Of all the herbs, only chives and sorrel really benefit from a yearly addition of compost or manure around the base of the plants. Chives, thyme varieties and sage have such pretty flowers that I placed these in my perennial flower bed. I often dig a small clump of chives in the fall and place it in my cold frame until it is too cold and then bring it in to winter on the windowsill. By the end of January I can begin cutting the tasty leaves.

Our garden is full of interesting rocks and so we planted thyme around some of the landscaping rocks in the perennial bed, where it softens the base of the rock and adds an attractive color. Another friend has used thyme and lavender to edge the base of her greenhouse much the same way you would use juniper plantings.

Herbs grow very well in our short but intense Montana summer and provide beauty as well as spice. Drying and freezing allows us to use them all year, but one of the best ways to use them in winter is to grow those able to survive our low winter light on the windowsill. ❧

A Lavender for All Reasons

Robert Kourik

My love affair with lavender began during the California drought of 1977 as a matter of necessity. As the planting portion of my business shriveled from lack of water, I began looking for drought-hardy plants to work with. The drought, by taking its toll on established landscapes, slowly revealed, like a grim version of time-lapse photography, which plants could best take the neglect and still look reasonably attractive—and lavenders were one of the champions. *Lavandula* sp. has become a love of mine and one of the three most important plants in my landscape design "palette." (The other two are rosemary and santolina.)

Since I have always lived in "wild" areas on the fringe of urban communities, deer browsing has always been a big concern of mine. Oddly enough, as a very general rule, native California plants are not that deer-resistant in a domesticated landscape setting —especially an irrigated one. It's the Mediterranean plants and, more specifically, the lavenders, which have proven to be most reliable at staying off the Bambi menu. After 15 years of landscaping in deer-browsing territory, I can state from observation that lavender plants remain virtually untouched.

Robert Kourik is a landscape designer who lives and gardens in Occidental, California. His specialty is edible landscaping, and he has written for many magazines, including Organic Gardening, Fine Gardening *and* Horticulture. *He is the author of* Designing and Maintaining Your Edible Landscape Naturally.

Planted correctly in the proper soil and climate, lavenders can easily be sustained with as few as two irrigations during an entire rainless California summer. The larger, shrubby lavenders act as effective weed suppressants since their two- to four-foot-tall canopy shades out germinating seeds. Equally important, lavenders require very limited shearing to maintain a pleasant and attractive form. All of this saves on the cost and time of installation and maintenance.

The "three D's" (drought, deer and dollars) are my most important *practical* reasons for planting lavenders. But the reasons I have for loving, collecting and growing so many forms of lavender around my house have to do with aesthetic and sensual virtues. The wide range of foliage and flower color, the seductive variety of sweet-pungent fragrances, the tantalizing possibilities of use for cooking, grilling and making ice cream tickle my fancy, my tastebuds and my creativity.

Soil Preparation

Contrary to regular garden practice, I always amend my small planting mounds for lavenders with the addition of plenty of gravel. Drainage is so critical to lavenders that, in any form of a clay loam, the addition of gravel, sand or a similar non-nitrogen amendment for drainage is absolutely *essential*. When in doubt about the drainage of a particular garden soil, amend raised planting

mounds or plant in a container filled with a well-drained potting mix. The single most important lesson when gardening in Mediterranean ecosystems is that providing the essential drainage is not only critical but makes for *better* plant growth; and at the same time, the *watering* needs are *not increased*, they may actually be *reduced*.

My Favorite Lavenders

My little list of favorite lavenders is based on the most common "trade" names, as used by the local wholesale nursery growers. This list comes from 10 years of using lavenders in landscaping and, more importantly, cultivating nearly two-dozen varieties around my home. *Photo by Elvin McDonald*

Photos by Robert Kourik

Lavendula angustifolia *is one of many lavender species that perform well in the author's California garden. These plants also have the distinct advantage of being deer-proof.*

Scent-sational

When it comes to the sweetest, best-scented, most-pungent lavender debate, I throw my Greek fisherman's hat into the *L. angustifolia* 'Provence' circle. I got my first plant from Louie and Virginia Saso in Saratoga, CA. The Sasos have been collecting herbs, landscaping their home with herbal gardens, teaching herb crafts and growing and selling organic herb plants for many decades, and I've been making yearly pilgrimages to this delightful herbal mecca for nearly 15 years. When Louie said 'Provence' was the finest-scented, sweetest-smelling, most-aromatic of all lavenders he's grown, I bought one instantly, and I think he's right. Sarah Hammond of Smith & Hawken's nursery also includes 'Provence' in her list of most powerfully scented lavenders. It has very fat flowers, nearly an inch in diameter, at the top one and a half to two inches of each stem. The flowers are so luxuriant and heavy that overhead irrigation, even heavy fog, can temporarily knock them over.

Colorful Lavender Blossoms

For sheer drama and rich color of blossom, my vote goes to *L. stoechas*, correctly called French lavender but sold as Spanish lavender around here. In the linguistic gymnastics of *Hortus Third*, the flowers are "oblong-obovate, to 2 in. long, verticillasters 6-10 -fld., calyx to 25 in. long, 13-nerved, corolla dark purple." (!) What excites me is the spectacularly rich, royal purple "flags" that stand

The lovely spikes of blooming lavender add fragrance to the air and beauty to the garden. Lavenders work well as small, discreet hedges.

straight up from the top of the flower. The beauty of French lavender has inspired me to spend considerable time reviving my long-lost love of super-closeup floral photography in an attempt to capture the naked, abstract "essence" of the blossom. My favorite-named variety for these floral "nude studies" is *L. stoechas* 'Atlas'. This one has by far the tallest,

L. stoechas *produces spectacular rich, royal purple "flags" that stand straight up from the top of the flower. The plant shape is well behaved, which reduces shearing.*

most regal "flags." Again, I found my first "model" at the Sasos' landscape nursery. A close contender for bud size is *L. stoechas* 'Otto Quest', which is much more prevalent in the average wholesale and retail nurseries. The species (unnamed selections or seed-grown plants) form of the French lavender has dramatically smaller blossoms, only up to five-eighths of an inch compared to the three-quarter- to one-inch-long buds of 'Otto Quest' and the nearly one and one-half inch buds of 'Atlas'. The advantage to the species form is its well-behaved plant shape and reduced shearing demands. And again, re-

member that those plants selected for huge blossoms flop over easily and can't take overhead irrigation or rain.

For a subtlety of color that is cool, relaxing and so delicate, I use the unique *L. angustifolia* 'Jean Davis'. This somewhat petite lavender has small, pale pink blossoms on slender stems. Some people refer to the bloom as white, but it's most accurately described as a creamy, pastel pink of the most delicate shade. The foliage, with a typical gray-green lavender color, and blossoms fit quite nicely with designs that feature silver-gray and dark green foliage and white or royal purple and blue blossoms. One particularly nice mixture is *L.* 'Jean Davis' in the foreground with rivulets of the more richly pink, gossamerlike blooms of Mexican evening primrose (*Oenothera berlandieri*) flowing behind and around the lavender. The plant seems a touch delicate, not able to take the same amount of neglect as most lavenders.

Low-Maintenance Lavenders

As mentioned above, the "three 'S's"— Spanish, Sweet and Spike lavenders—offer

L. angustifolia *'Jean Davis' has small, pale pink blossoms on slender stems. The plant is delicate and combines nicely with* Oenothera berlandieri.

more low-maintenance benefits to any landscape than even most other lavenders. The true French lavender is not tall enough to shade out all germinating seeds, but needs very little shearing to stay in a compact, half-spherical form.

Landscape Design with Lavender in Mind

I have, or make, many occasions to add lavenders to the plans of my clients, mainly to help create what I call drifts or swales of color for the primary "wash" of the design. I think of garden design as a process resembling a watercolor painting, the first step being to lay down a pale "wash" (thin liquid color) of primary, background color against which main highlights and accents will appear.

Many of the natural plants in the California chaparral grow in fairly large, pure stands due to their physiological competitiveness (such as when they give off allelopathic chemicals that stunt the growth of other plants or prevent the germination of their seeds), so I create portions of my designs to reflect this pattern. The soft tones of blue-gray, glaucous, and green-foliaged lavenders fit nicely with my vision of a natural chaparral look. Like the evergreen chaparral, the foliage of lavender provides an intriguing, but not too intense, color all year, regardless of the season. By planting large clusters of lavender on top of raised mounds in meandering patterns, I intend to mimic the image of the large, oddly shaped pools of single-species plants that are often found in chaparral communities.

Since it is rare that chaparral communities are composed of entirely silver-gray, glaucous-foliaged plants, I often turn to dark green evergreen plants, which provide an interesting foil or counterpoint to the lavender, making the silver-gray leaves look lighter colored and enhancing their blue tones. Conversely, the lavender's foliage makes the evergreen's foliage look even richer and deeper. For these dark-green foils, some of the plants I use include: *Myoporum parvifolium* 'Pink', rosemary (*Rosmarinus officinalis*), sticky monkey flower (*Mimulus* sp.) and common thyme (*Thymus vulgaris*). Often, I place the low-growing *Myoporum parvifolium* 'Pink' or common thyme beneath a lavender to grow out from under its foliage like a dark green skirt, setting off the gray-green foliage above.

Lavender naturally grows in a well-behaved, mounding form. This soft, half-spherical shape becomes a welcome contrast to straight structural lines on the house or in the landscape. A four-foot-tall lavender, combined with several other rounded shrubs, can be used to soften the edges or corners of a house. I most frequently use lavenders as small, discreet hedges to hide the straight, wooden edges of raised vegetable beds. Because gophers are so prevalent in our area, raised beds with wooden sides and aviary-wire bottoms are essential to a garden's survival. The hard line and rigid geometry of these boxes has always troubled me as a designer; sometimes I just celebrate the geometry, even making it more prominent, as an intentional design theme. Otherwise, I often use sweeping hedges of lavender to soften the architectural nature of the beds. In one landscaping job, the wooden boxes were placed perpendicular to a large gradual curve, facing south. Along the southern edge, I planted a long hedge of *L. angustifolia* to match the sweeping curve. As the lavender never gets above 18 to 24 inches, it doesn't significantly shade the vegetables, and does some nice things besides softening the boxy look. It separates the lawn area from the food-growing area, hides the irrigation pipes that enter from the southern sides of the bed, sweetens the garden atmosphere—especially when in bloom—provides fresh flowers for bouquets, cooking and grilling, keeps the bees well-fed, makes a striking accent when in full flower and attracts many beneficial insects to its flowers. ✥

BORDERLINE HERBS

A choice handful equally useful in border or kitchen

Ann Lovejoy

We could never find room in our tiny city garden for a real herb garden, but there are a few culinary plants we couldn't do without. Given thoughtful treatment, most herbs perform very nicely in a mixed border, and some are so lovely that I would grow them even if we didn't enjoy their flavors. Here are a few of the outstanding basics which are both savory and beautiful for most of the year.

Finocchio, or Florence fennel, is a great favorite of mine, not only for the fat "bulbs" that form at the base of this billowy plant, but for the aromatic, plumy foliage. It is not unlike dill, but thicker, and softer in effect. A well-grown plant will make a dense, columnar bush fully six or even eight feet high and nearly three feet across at its middle. Does that sound like too much of a good thing? At ground level, it really takes up very little room, and can be planted where the emerging foliage will first mingle with, then cover up the fading leaves of spring bulbs. It is a great mistake to worry too much about scale in a small garden, and a few oversized gems like this will bring you enormous pleasure. When wet, this great spangled thing glitters like a fountain, each drooping leaflet carrying a shimmering silver drop. In the fall it colors warmly, taking on tints of copper and bronze. By midwinter it has lost a good deal of its charm, but when the old stalks are cut down a whole fluffy wealth of new greenery is already on its way up, and very welcome

it is, too. I grow a small row of fennel plants in the vegetable garden as well, where they take up very little room; there they are grown as annuals and harvested fairly small, just as the bulbs fatten up. My big border fennel is four years old and still going strong.

There is a pretty variety of the common fennel (the one that does not make big "bulbs"), which has foliage of bronze or copper. This makes a comparatively smaller plant, perhaps three feet tall, slim and airy. This can be planted in small thickets of three or four plants as a splendid background for flaming red *Cosmos* 'Diablo', daylilies, whether the smoldering red-black 'American Revolution' or fiery crimson 'Cup of Rubies', cinnamon red 'Pirate' lilies or the old fashioned red hot poker, *Kniphofia (Tritoma) uvaria*. A subtler effect, equally wonderful in a quiet way, comes from bronze fennel banked with apricot and peach-toned daylilies, 'Three Bars' and 'Knockout', and another *Kniphofia* 'Primrose Beauty', this one with lily-wands of pale yellow. Several single plants can be tucked about in a small shrub border for a pleasant deepening tone and light feeling. In the herb garden, try it with purple-leaved perilla, that cinnamony-basil flavored herb so often used in Japanese cooking, and the lemon-lime form of cooking sage or fluffy golden marjoram. Even without flowers this group is spectacular, in the very best sense of the word.

Allium schoenoprasum, *chives, grows in most gardens and graces them with fat purple flower balls that look especially pretty when backed by the fuzzy silver leaves of lamb's ears.*

Most gardens have some chives, and the long-blooming, fat purple flower balls look especially pretty when backed by the fuzzy silver leaves and tall purple and silver towers of lamb's ears. Chives have a more elegant cousin which is less often grown, though just as easy to please, and far more useful in a mixed border. This is garlic chives, *Allium tuberosum*, the flowers white in a wide and delicate umbel. They also bloom for a long time and smell quite sweet unless bruised or cut. We have them fetchingly sandwiched between a low sprawling rose, 'The Fairy', with small pink pompom flowers for much of the year, and a pink jasmine. Garlic chives will seed themselves around a bit, yet they are so attractive, and so easily removed if not wanted they are never a nuisance.

Parsley is such a pretty plant that I grow it in its several forms even though we rarely cook with it. The flat Italian kind is useful in vases with smallish cut flowers, lasting very well, and the plants bring that fresh, lively color and light texture to our small shrub and bulb border. The frizzy, crimped types are as much fun to use as the various dusty millers, and the two together can make an uninspired planting hum with energy. An ordinary hanging basket of scented purple and pink petunias needs only a few additions to be something quite special; a tumbling white pansy (a climber going the wrong way), some ruffled parsley and the lacy silver dusty miller 'Diamond' will turn it into a complex and lively grouping.

Clearly there are many ways to get a few herbs into the act without giving them a proper bed of their own. Thymes of all sorts are evergreen and always attractive, whether creeping or clumping, green or gold or gray. Feathery dill and lacy lovage lighten heavy foliage in shrub borders. Dramatic angelica looks wonderful behind billowing perennials. Blue-flowered borage blends with other self-sowing annuals in bright abundance. Silvery lavender, bushy rosemary and cut-leaved tarragon can all be introduced to mixed company without any fuss or worry. Nestled in with all the border beauties, these humble escapees from the kitchen garden look good enough to eat. The only difficulty is getting them out of their beds and into the kitchen. 🦋

Parsley is such a pretty plant with a fresh, lively color and light texture that it is a pleasant addition even if not used in cooking. There are several types to choose from.

TEA LEAVES

Herbs to blend and brew

Patrick Lima

L arkwhistle garden grows a score or more of tea herbs. An essential step in the tea ceremony here—at least during the seven-month growing season—is to take the teapot into the garden and fill it loosely with an impromptu blend of fresh herb leaves and sometimes flowers or seeds as well. One morning it will be a citrus-sweet mixture of lemon balm, lemon verbena and anise-hyssop leaves, with sprigs of spearmint and unripe seeds of sweet cicely. Another day it

A few flowers can be added to tea blends. Pictured here are sprays of lavender—the florets can be floated in herbal teas. Floating on the surface is a lovage flower.

Photos by Elvin McDonald

Tea made from mint is stimulating and refreshing. The plants are easy to grow, but must be contained so that they do not invade the entire garden. Tea made from sage is milder and is said to have medicinal benefits.

will be a tonic, slightly bitter brew of sage combined with a bit of rosemary, a smidgen of rue and a few flower heads of common yarrow. A favorite blend has lemon balm, spearmint and orange mint as the dominant flavors, with a leaf of sage and a sprig of rosemary and a few leaves of anise-hyssop or sweet cicely for sweetness. Into the pot may go calendula flowers, the fragrant petals of old-fashioned roses, leaves of scented geraniums or spikes of flowering lavender. In the evening we have a sleepy tea of catnip leaves and chamomile flowers with a little mint to temper the medicinal edge. Sometimes I brew a bouillonlike tea of parsley, lovage, savory, dill seeds, chive blossoms, thymes or other

Patrick Lima and his partner, John Scanlan, live and work in their beautiful garden, Larkwhistle, in Ontario, Canada. Lima has written extensively for Harrowsmith *magazine, and his books include* The Harrowsmith Perennial Garden: Flowers For Three Seasons *and* The Harrowsmith Illustrated Book of Herbs.

potherbs salted with a few drops of tamari or a daub of miso paste.

Blends vary with the seasons—summer teas often include lemon or cinnamon basil or leaves of the tender tropical sages or a bit of one of the milder-scented geraniums. Seldom is one pot of herb tea just like another. But besides their endless variety, herb teas have a lot going for them. They are homegrown and hence can be free from the pesticides and other chemicals routinely used in the raising, processing, packing and shipping of commercial herbs. They cost nothing beyond a small sum for seed or starter plants and, best of all, the plants themselves are among the easiest in the garden to grow.

Mint
Mentha spp, *Pycnanthemum pilosum*

Growing with such abandon that they need occasional restraining, some mints are distinctly pushy plants moving in on neighbors by surface runners or underground rhizomes. A few, however, are worth growing in corners of the garden where they will not menace other things. One member of the family, peppermint, makes the most familiar of all herb teas. But if the reaction of visitors to a whiff of the head-clearing fresh leaves in our garden is a clue, few gardeners know the true peppermint (*Mentha piperita*), which smells, as might be expected, like those red-and-white-striped Christmas candies or a peppermint patty—it is sometimes sold as candy mint. *M. piperita* may also be labelled black peppermint in reference to its purple-brown stems and top leaves suffused with deep violet. Still, it is wise to taste before buying. Even a nibble of true peppermint will fill the mouth with the characteristic mentholated coolness that identifies it.

Peppermint is a hybrid plant. "Seeds sold as peppermint," states one herb catalog, "are never true to name; quality strains can only be grown from cuttings or divisions." In our

garden peppermint is the least expansionist of mints; our small clump barely maintains itself in a corner of a raised bed where six other species jostle for root room. But in a neighbor's garden a slip from our plant has covered a wide swath of ground in the shade of some old apple trees. Peppermint craves partial shade, good black loam and moisture —one parent is water mint (*Mentha aquatica*), a vigorous plant that grows beside streams throughout Europe.

"Peppermint will stimulate like a glass of whiskey," Jethro Kloss says in his book of herbal medicine, *Back to Eden*. An overstatement, but there is no doubt that strong peppermint tea is a potent drink. I have heard several people say that they cannot take their mint tea strong and straight—"it goes right through me." All the herbals agree that the active constituents of peppermint act on the organs of digestion; the tea (or oil, which contains about 50 percent menthol) is recommended to allay stomach cramps, nausea, abdominal pains and the like.

Peppermint's other parent, spearmint, is far more common in gardens. It can be distinguished from peppermint by its leaves, which are uniformly green, pebbled, longer, more pointed and toothed along their margins—spiked, in fact, as the Latin *Mentha spicata* tells us—while peppermint leaves are smooth-edged. Southerners call it julep mint; alternate names, lamb mint and pea mint, indicate that this is the plant for general culinary use in sauces and jellies or minced over boiled potatoes, steamed carrots or fresh peas. A little spearmint clipped into green, grain or potato salads dressed with yogurt is a cooling touch. The scent and flavor of spearmint, milder than peppermint, blends well with other tea herbs, such as balm, anisehyssop or chamomile, whereas peppermint would overpower them.

A pretty sport of spearmint is curly mint (*Mentha spicata* 'Crispata'), whose leaves are twisted, waved and crimped along the edges. Gardeners with limited space might grow curly mint in preference to its parent for the

Excerpted with permission from The Harrowsmith Illustrated Book of Herbs sake of its decorative foliage. I have noticed, too, that curly mint never succumbs to the spotty fungus disease that sometimes bothers other species.

Different from other mints is one with the fragrance of eau de Cologne. Orange mint (*Mentha citrata*) is also called bergamot mint because of its resemblance to *Monarda didyma*. Too perfumed, for my taste, to make a good tea on its own, a few sprigs of orange mint will add a unique bouquet to a blend that may include lemon balm and anise-hyssop. Attached by short stalks to the square stems typical of all mints are broadly heart-shaped leaves; these and the unusual fragrance identify orange mint.

For sheer beauty of leaf, no mint can match the variegated form of apple mint (*Mentha* x *rotundifolia variegata*), also called pineapple mint. Apple-green, woolly rounded leaves smelling of apples and spice are flecked and bordered with creamy white. Not as determined a spreader as some, apple mint is an easy herb for massing in a lightly shaded corner of a city (or any) garden where height —about three feet—and highlights are needed. I have seen it given a prominent place toward the front of English perennial beds as an effective foliage accent.

Equally decorative is golden ginger mint (*Mentha* x *gentilis aureo-variegata*), sometimes called American apple mint. (Given the many and similar common names, it is easy to see how useful the Latin can be.) Smaller, serrated (botanically called toothed or dentate) green leaves are shot through with yellow and cream. To my nose the scent resembles tangerines. In our garden a clump of American apple mint grows at the side of a concrete watering pool, where it seems to appreciate the shade and dampness.

Mints are the easiest plants to propagate— and, in fact, are more likely to need curbing. Any shoot eased from the ground is likely to have a few roots. Planted firmly in a new place, it soon takes hold and starts to travel. Gardeners go to great lengths to confine mints: sinking sheets of metal, even used license plates, around a patch; hauling old tires into the garden; planting in containers of all sorts. Wooden wine-barrel halves are my choice for mints and most other herbs because they are not porous like clay, so far less watering is required—nor have I ever seen clay pots as large. A half-barrel will contain three species of mint comfortably. But each spring, the tangled mat of roots that will fill a barrel in a season must be pried and pulled out just as growth begins, and three to five shoots of each type replanted. If a single species grows in a half-barrel, it can be left for several seasons.

With mints one can have one's tea and bathe in it too: the long branches of any fresh mints (but especially orange and peppermint) swished vigorously back and forth in a tub of hot water, then left to swirl under the faucet, make a fragrant bath; or simply empty a teapot full of a strong, minty brew into the tub. The practice is an old one. John Parkinson, apothecary to King James I and author of two 17th-century herbal classics, wrote, "Mints are sometimes used in the bath with balm and other herbs to comfort and strengthen the nerves and sinews." Since mint is a reputed anodyne—an agent that soothes pain—and is also recommended to relieve itching skin conditions, a mint bath may be as therapeutic as it is pleasant.

Far too small to be easily picked for tea, let alone a bath, the ground-hugging half-inch-tall Corsican mint (*Mentha requienii*) is nevertheless a sweet plant that will creep between paving stones or carpet a shaded slope of the rock garden, if it is not harassed by stronger plants. This herb has the tiniest flowers of any plant in the garden—a little pale lavender galaxy—but honeybees crawl eagerly over the small-leaved mats. Native to a warm Mediterranean island, Corsican mint is not as easy as some to keep over the winter —the herb lady who sold us a starter plant pronounced it "definitely tender"—but under the snow, small patches always squeak through and grow over the summer to fill in the bare places. A springy mulch of evergreen boughs (not matted leaves) is recommended protection where freeze and thaw is the winter pattern. Some gardeners recommend removing the mats of Corsican mint to a cold frame or even indoors over winter, but I confess that my interest in a plant wanes if I have to move it twice a year. Only the decidedly tender rosemary, lemon verbena and several tropical sages (all good tea herbs) receive that attention.

Despite its name, mountain mint (*Pycnanthemum pilosum* or *Koellia pilosa*), a hardy American native, is not a species of mint at all, although it is a member of the same family, Labiatae, to which mint, bergamot and several other herbs belong. Its crushed leaves are redolent of peppermint and may be used in the same ways. Three-foot-high mountain mint does not creep but returns each spring wider by just a shoot or two. Nectar-hungry insects are drawn to the dowdy whitish flowers; I have counted four species of butterflies feeding at once, as well as a bevy of bees and smaller flying things. The flowers must brim with an unusually sweet nectar. Grow this plant from spring-sown seed or starter plants; our specimen lives in sandy ground in full sun but would probably respond to soil enrichment with more lush growth.

Chamomile
Chamaemelum nobile, Matricaria recutita

A sprinkling of seed scratched lightly into any piece of sunny ground in spring will provide chamomile in perpetuity. What you sow, you reap. The choice is between the creeping perennial Roman chamomile (*Chamaemelum nobile* or *Anthemis nobilis*), a colonizing species that grows so thickly it has been used as a ground cover for paths or as a lawn substitute—"so that being trod upon, the scent is set free to regale and invigorate the passerby," wrote one gardener—and the annual German wild or sweet-false-chamomile (*Matricaria recutita* or *M. chamomilla*), sometimes judged better for tea.

I grow annual chamomile, or rather it has grown itself for years, with no attention ex-

Chamomile
Matricaria recutita

cept thinning (to three or four inches apart) the dense crop of fine-leaved seedlings that springs up every season and weeding out their increasing kind from the paths (maybe I should leave them) or from the crowns of pinks and dwarf catnip edging a bed opposite. It is wise to grow chamomile (both the self-seeding German and the creeping Roman) in the vegetable garden—perhaps at the end of an intensive bed or in the corner where seedlings may remain undisturbed. Grown anywhere near other small herbs or perennials, seedlings become a nuisance, lodging where they will.

In preparing chamomile tea, remember that it is easy to oversteep the flowers past pleasant and fruity to bitter; equal parts chamomile and spearmint or lemon balm leaves make a more mellow brew, and a scant teaspoon of dried chamomile makes a cup of tea. Once dubbed "the plant physician," chamomile produces one of the most venerable herbal brews, long popular in the home medicine chest to soothe and strengthen stomachs and to calm restless or feverish children. In her book, *A Modern Herbal*, published in 1931, Maud Grieve says of the plant, "It has a wonderfully soothing, sedative and absolutely harmless effect." This is another herb tea to pour into bathwater; a little can be reserved for rinsing the hair to bring out highlights.

Chamomile has a reputed influence not only upon "frail humanity in distress," as one herbalist put it, but also upon other plants; grown near "weak or ailing plants, it exerts a strengthening influence." Cooled tea sprayed over a flat of seedlings, or dried chamomile flowers scattered between them, is said to reduce the risk of damping-off, a fungus that can lay low a batch of small plants in short order.

There is but one difficulty in growing chamomile: harvesting the flowers is like picking wild strawberries—it takes forever to fill a teapot or to gather enough to pack dry into a jar for winter teas. This is work for a sunny Sunday when one is content to sit in the chamomile patch, under the shade of a wide-brimmed hat, and just pick. We harvest chamomile flowers first when the patch looks to be in full flower, taking small button buds, the wide-open flowers and everything in between. Soon, this generous herb is full of blooms again; three or four successive pickings are possible if patience, ever a virtue in gardening, persists. To dry chamomile flowers for tea, spread them in a single layer on a screen in an airy, shaded place out of the way of rain or dew, stirring and turning every few days until the flowers appear desiccated. Then store for a while in a punctured paper bag to ensure that drying is complete, lest the bulky flowers mold in closed jars.

Bergamot
Monarda spp.
Goodness and moisture, too, are needed for

Monarda didyma, another herb of many names—bergamot, bee-balm, monarda, Oswego tea. This is a favorite of mine on several counts. The whole plant—flowers and leaves (and roots, says one writer, although I have not investigated that claim)—smells deliciously of oranges and spice; the leaves add a special bouquet to a tea blend, similar to the flowery essence that pervades Earl Grey tea.

Bergamot is a North American native. In 1744, so the story goes, Virginia farmer and amateur botanist John Bartram collected seeds from stands of red bergamot found growing near Oswego, New York—both the town and the tea received their names from the Oswego Indian tribe that lived in the region and apparently used several species of *Monarda* to flavor their food. Bartram sent seeds to English horticulturist Peter Collinson who recorded that "plants flowered the next year, and by 1760, there were plenty in Covent Garden Market." Two centuries later, there are plenty in this garden, too, and I wouldn't want it otherwise.

Crowns of tubular flowers, sometimes one atop the other, may be shades of purple or rose-pink. For curious gardeners, seeds of the 'Panorama' strain will flower in a range of colors the first season. But better are the named varieties of plants: 'Croftway Pink' is one cultivar to look for, and best of all is the glowing red 'Cambridge Scarlet', always alive with hummingbirds performing their aerial acrobatics. Bergamot colors for weeks in July and early August. Each season, I find a new corner that would be brighter for a plant of bergamot, perhaps behind a cloud of baby's-breath or in front of the reaching spires of delphinium or dusky blue aconite. With tall lilies and day lilies of any color, three-to-four-foot-tall red bergamot makes a fiery picture.

Bergamot is amiable enough if its few specific needs are met. Give it organically enriched ground that does not dry out, or it will lose its lower leaves and become stunted. Give it elbowroom and good air circulation, or it will become lanky and mildewed. Divide it first thing in spring or early in autumn, or it will spread, mintlike, into a choked mat of weak shoots. Division is easy—all the roots are near the surface—but the gardener must ruthlessly toss out the spent center of the clump and retain three-shoot segments from the outside as new plants. Set these firmly, and a little deeper than they were growing, in the best ground you can manage in sun or partial shade. Thus treated, bergamot will be the jewel of the July garden, and its leaves will make many a cup of fragrant tea.

The delicate lavender flowers of wild bergamot (*Monarda fistulosa*) decorate roadsides, thickets and clearings throughout parts of eastern Canada and New England. At one time, native people steeped the leaves into a medicinal tea for mild fevers, headaches, colds and sore throats; other herbalists speak of bergamot, a general tonic, as a specific for stomach ailments. The genus is named for Spanish medical botanist Nicholas de Monardes, author of a book pleasantly titled *Joyfull Newes out of the Newe Founde Worlde*.

Anise-Hyssop
Agastache foeniculum

Although it is little known and seldom grown, anise-hyssop is good company for balm in both the garden and the teapot. This three-to-four-foot-tall easy plant, always surrounded by honeybees and butterflies when in flower, ought to have a place toward the back of a bed of tea herbs. Leaves scented of anise and mint—licorice-mint is another common name—clothe square stems topped with short but showy spires of bright lavender flowers. If hung upside down in an airy, shaded place, the flower spikes dry as easily as yarrow for a winter bouquet. Since the shrivelled leaves are not decorative, they can be stripped for tea.

Just once have I seen these plants for sale; and anise-hyssop does not spread by runners as do plants of the genus *Mentha*. But spring-sown seed grows usable anise-hyssop in a season; left to seed, it scatters a colony of young plants at its feet. In hot, starved soil, this hungry herb grows stunted and weedy-looking, but given moisture and goodness (old manure, compost, peat moss and the like), anise-hyssop is an ornamental that provides weeks of late-summer color and months of fresh licorice-mint leaves for tea.

Costmary
Chrysanthemum balsamita

In old abandoned farm gardens near my home, costmary has stood its ground against encroaching field flowers and grasses for half a century or more. My elderly neighbors know the herb as "sweet Mary," but none can recall just what their parents or grandparents used it for—"probably tea" is the usual guess.

A close botanical relative of the feathery, dark green tansy (*Tanacetum vulgare* syn. *Chrysanthemum vulgare*), costmary, in contrast, grows smooth, elongated, oval leaves, toothed along their edges and lightly silvered with a coating of countless minute hairs. Its flowering stems support clusters of small, yellow tansylike button flowers (actually the central disc of a composite or daisy flower minus the surrounding florets) on three-to-five-foot stems. Given costmary's persistence in old gardens, it is no surprise that the herb takes to sun or light shade, dry or moist ground and forms an enduring clump in a season or two.

To my nose, the scent of costmary is a mixture of mint and wormwood, an aroma once described as "vaguely reminiscent of 'morning bitters', whiskey with bitter herbs." Bitterness is all that comes through if costmary is nibbled, yet the herb was once included in every "Sabbath posy," a nosegay of aromatic leaves and flowers carried by churchgoers to amuse the nose and titillate the taste buds during drawn-out sermons. At meeting's end, the long leaves were tucked between the pages of the Good Book, a custom reflected in the name Bible leaf.

Today, this stalwart old herb, "once very common in all gardens," according to a 16th-century writer—and amusingly listed as "new for '86" in a recent herb catalog—is appreciated (again) by herb-tea fanciers for the balsamic bite it gives to a blend of milder herbs. The licorice sweetness of anise-hyssop or sweet cicely, or the citrus taste of any of the leafy lemons—balm, verbena, thyme and geranium—all temper costmary's edge. In any case, the bitterness of a nibbled leaf is considerably mellowed by several minutes' brewing. Ordinary black tea can be spiced with a bit of costmary (and any other tea herb for that matter). But, like the early New World settlers, I sometimes enjoy a cup of costmary tea straight.

Horehound
Marrubium spp.

If costmary can be pleasant on its own in tea, horehound cannot. Whether brewed or chewed, this is a bitter herb that tastes as if it just might be as good a medicine as it has been reputed to be. An infusion of horehound is meant to remedy a weak stomach or lack of appetite, while horehound tea, syrup or candies have alleviated coughs, colds and sore throats for many centuries.

In our garden woolly, silver-green tufts of horehound appear here and there, like catnip; grown originally from seed, it can be counted on to naturalize itself. It is pretty enough for a corner of a flower bed—its two-foot height can be attractive in dry places where other plants are reluctant to grow.

Roses
Rosa spp.

Among the most exotic flowers for the teapot are roses, although it is the fruit of the rose—the vitamin-C-rich hip, or hep—that is most often brewed. The species *Rosa rugosa* and its many named selections produce some of the biggest and most prolific hips. Unlike modern hybrid tea roses, lanky prima donnas which demand that a gardener keep them warm in winter, fend off pests that might annoy them and generally keep them in good health, rugosa roses flourish even in sandy ground, are ignored by insects of all sorts and

are hardy without protection even in the northlands and on the prairies. Rugosa is a rose that yields fragrant flowers from mid-June through July, then opens a blossom or two until September when it regains a rosy fall glow.

Why doesn't every garden grow at least one bush of *Rosa rugosa*? Perhaps the tag "shrub rose" has frightened some gardeners who envisage a space grabber, but this prickly beauty needs less room than a suckering lilac or a straggling (and none-too-hardy) forsythia. Some gardeners feel that any rose more exuberant than a spindly hybrid tea has gone wild—and indeed, *Rosa rugosa* has created weedy thickets in parts of New England and farther south—or that a rose is only a rose if its petals spiral formally into a tight, high-centered blossom, beside which the blowsy rugosa bloom seems not quite elegant. The color of the wild rugosa rose is magenta, sporting simple, open, five-petalled flowers. Let us call the rugosa flowers informal and appreciate the plant's many good qualities.

Canadian hybridizers have always been keen on improving the Japanese native *Rosa rugosa* as well as the numerous wild single-flowered rose species that grow across the country. During the 1920s, in Ottawa, Isabel Preston turned her considerable skill from lilacs, lilies and the Siberian iris to *Rosa rugosa* and left as a legacy a willowy (to five feet) amber-cream cultivar named 'Agnes'. More recently, gene jugglers in Morden, Manitoba, and in Ottawa have introduced a bevy of hardy beauties, many of which have double blooms—that is, flowers with at least twice the normal number of petals.

Along a 75-foot stretch of rail fence, we have planted a selection of rugosa hybrids. The two fall days given to digging holes (18 inches deep and wide), removing subsoil, piling in a nourishing mixture of old manure, topsoil, peat moss and bone meal, well stirred with a spading fork, and finally setting in the stripling bushes have yielded perennial returns in flowers, fragrance and fruit. The dense hedge also buffers westerly winds that would otherwise chill the vegetable garden.

If one is after a crop of rose hips for tea, the rugosa roses are among the best, but understand that not all cultivars are created equal. 'Martin Frobisher', listed as a rugosa hybrid, produces no fruit in this garden, nor does 'Agnes'. 'Hansa', six to eight feet tall, well known and overly vigorous in most gardens, has loose wine-colored flowers and only a few large hips. 'Jens Munk', five to six feet tall, opens pure pink semidouble flowers followed by lots of marble-sized crimson hips. Most productive of large, orange-red hips is 'Scabrosa', a restrained and elegant four-foot shrub carrying wide-open single flowers, mallow-pink with a center of creamy stamens. Of those we grow, the latter two are my choices for hip production.

Pick rose hips when they are plump and red but not softly over-ripe; trim the stem and blossom end, cut the hips in half, scoop out the seeds and fibers with a small spoon, and dry the halves on a screen in an airy, shaded place indoors. Dried rose hips are as hard as coffee beans; to make tea, pulverize a handful in a blender, grinder or mill and steep for at least 10 minutes with other herbs, dry or fresh, for more flavor.

Lemon Balm
Melissa officinalis

"Comforts the heart and driveth away melancholy and sadness," wrote English herbalist John Gerard of balm, in the 16th century. Almost every potful of fresh herbs I pick for tea includes a generous helping of lemon balm leaves. Few herbs are as sweetly cordial —the scent is citrus but not sharp, much like the bland, refreshing *limón dulce*, or sweet lemon, eaten like an orange in Mexico and points south. Here is the perfect tea herb. The mild flavor blends well with all other herbs; it offends no taste buds; and the plant, a completely hardy perennial, grows willingly in any good ground, in sun or shade. True, lemon balm is a mover, but much less so than mints; three clumps have been in place in our dryish garden for seven years with no tampering or attention. Its spread—faster in rich, moist earth—is easily checked with a sharp trowel; and if the maturing seed stalks are cut back, no seedlings will spring up. Two plants will meet most needs, but beekeepers might want more.

Melissa is Greek for bee; *Melissa officinalis*, "medicinal bee," is the botanical tag for lemon balm. Balm and honeybees belong together. Not only do the worker bees seek balm nectar, but leaves rubbed all over a hive seem to calm a colony that has just endured the trauma of a trip through the mail. In preparation for working with our bees, my partner, John Scanlan, rubs his hands with balm and brushes his clothing with the branches—better safe than sorry. This little ritual slows him down and, one hopes, makes the bees take more kindly to the intrusion. I read that the Greeks once stuffed their skeps —those picturesque beehives made of coiled straw—with branches of balm in hopes of attracting a passing swarm.

Balm is just as appealing to humans. In all herbal literature, the plant is described as soothing and useful for "nervous problems, hysteria, melancholy and insomnia." Equal parts of lemon balm, chamomile and catnip make an effective nightcap tea; balm, mint and anise-hyssop create a delicious breakfast brew.

Fresh balm leaves also add a mild citrus tang to green salads or other light summer dishes. My preference is fresh balm for tea as well; the flavor, subtle even when fresh, barely survives drying (although we dry a few branches for a winter blend). In any case, fresh frost-hardy balm can be harvested during at least half the year here, longer on the "balmy" West Coast.

Others

Herbs which I like to add to a blend in lesser quantities or brew alone as a medicinal tea, include:

Rue (*Ruta graveolens*): Use the fresh

leaves, a tiny smidgen only because of the bitterness and because rue, although beneficial if properly used, is powerful; large doses are capable of producing mental confusion and can even be toxic. Rue is an abortifacient and so should not be consumed at all by pregnant women. Also, handling the plant can cause allergic reactions in susceptible people.

Hyssop (*Hyssopus officinalis*): Bitter but decorative, hyssop, whose tea is also not recommended for continual use, is an old country remedy for rheumatism. A leaf gives body to a blend of sweet herbs.

Sage (*Salvia officinalis*): Fresh or dried, a little adds depth and highly praised health benefits to blends of milder-tasting herbs.

Mullein (*Verbascum* spp): Flowers, fresh or dried from wild or garden mulleins, add flavor and body to mixtures.

Catnip (*Nepeta cataria*): This produces a very soothing tea; sleep-inducing if strong, made from fresh or dried leaves alone or blended with chamomile, balm or mints. It tastes pleasant if sweetened with honey.

Chamomile tea is made by steeping dried leaves and flowers. Don't oversteep or the tea will turn from pleasant and fruity to bitter.

Lemon Thyme (*Thymus* x *citriodorus*): The fresh leaves have the scent and flavor of citrus and spice. Use other thymes for tea, as you like.

Sweet Cicely (*Myrrhis odorata*): This is an excellent tea herb, whose Latin name means "fragrant perfume." The leaves or crushed green seeds add sweetness and a taste of anise to a blend; used alone, sweet cicely tea is said to act as a "gentle stimulant for debilitated stomachs." The sweet seeds of anise or fennel, both of which taste of licorice, may also go into the teapot.

A few flowers can be added to the tea blends. Lavender (*Lavandula vera*) flowers perfume a mixture and, according to John Gerard's 16th-century herbal, are of "especially good use for all griefes of the head and brain and comforteth the stomach." Petals of the old-fashioned fragrant roses and the ray, or outside florets, or bright orange and yellow calendula (*Calendula officinalis*) are good for tea. Use flower florets fresh or dried.

The leaves and flowers of yarrow (*Achillea millefolium*), fresh or dried, were commonly brewed by North American native people

into a general health-building and digestion-aiding tonic. A good addition to a blend, yarrow also makes a pleasantly bitter and aromatic brew on its own, although large doses can produce headaches and vertigo. A mineral-rich tea made from the dried leaves of alfalfa (*Medicago sativa*) has been described as "helpful for every condition of the body, whether maintaining or regaining a healthy state." Blend bland alfalfa leaves with more aromatic mint, lemon balm, anise-hyssop and the like.

Wild Ingredients

The best source of rose hips may be a tangle of wild plants growing in a field or an empty lot beyond one's garden. Many of the native species have good-sized fruits, and the hips of all roses are edible, although not all are large or numerous enough to be worth seeking. Farther afield, meadows and woodlands provide other forage for herb tea aficionados. A tea made from wild strawberry leaves is a reputed "blood cleanser," while raspberry leaves brew a delicately flavored beverage with mild medicinal effects. Both of these are best blended with more aromatic herbs from the garden. A tea of red clover (*Trifolium pratense*), the ubiquitous pasture plant, is said to be very soothing to the nerves; gargled, a strong infusion helps soothe a sore, in-flamed throat.

Also blended for beverages is St. John's wort (*Hypericum perforatum*), a common roadside and meadow flower recognizable by its clusters of small but showy sunburst yellow flowers in late summer. The flowers and leafy tops of *Hypericum* species were once found in almost every Old World country household, where they were used medicinally, both externally and internally, to improve sleep, blood circulation and the working of the gastrointestinal system. Now, the plant is usually blended with other herbs simply for use as a beverage.

While it is a good mixer in a blend, yarrow also makes a pleasantly bitter and aromatic brew on its own. Mineral-rich alfalfa, on the other hand, is best blended with more fragrant mint, lemon balm, anise-hyssop and the like.

Tender Tea Herbs

"What does this smell like?" I asked a five-year-old visitor, tucking a crumpled leaf under his nose.

"Suckers," he said without hesitation and, after another sniff, "yellow suckers."

Of all the herbal lemons—lemon balm, thyme, basil, scented geraniums and verbena —the latter (*Lippia citriodora* now *Aloysia triphylla*) is the sweetest and the closest to the real thing. The trouble is that lemon verbena, a small shrub native to Chile and Peru, demands heat and full sun to flourish and shrivels at the first breath of frost. Two sweet-smelling tropical sages—the names pineapple sage (*Salvia elegans*) and fruit sage (*S. dorisiana*) say it all—also thrive in heat and sunlight but struggle and become spindly in low light and chilly places. It is best not to grow the tender herbs if conditions are wrong, but one is tempted for the sake of their ambrosial scents.

The tender tropicals are best grown in large (10 to 12-inch diameter) clay pots that can be shifted outdoors into the sun when summer has settled and brought in again before the first fall frost. The soil mix must be porous but nourishing and moisture-retentive without staying soggy. I like roughly equal parts of good garden loam (but not clay), sifted compost or bagged manure and perlite —several double handfuls of peat moss and a handful of bone meal are a help. Set small nursery plants directly into the large pots to get them going and to avoid time-consuming potting up later.

There are two options for wintering lemon verbena and the tender sages. Either keep them in active but slowed growth all winter by placing them in the sunniest place indoors—a south-facing bay window, sun-room, greenhouse or equivalent—or, lacking such a spot, store the tender herbs after their late fall pruning as one does geraniums, in a cool low-light place (by a basement window or in a protected shed), keeping the soil nearly, but not totally, dry. The herbs will be semi-dormant and need not be disturbed until about a month before the last spring frost, when they are brought again into warmth and light to gear up for summer. In either case, one never feeds a plant that is not actively growing. Potted herbs respond to a drink of half-strength fish emulsion, or the equivalent, two or three times from May through August only.

Pruning twice a year is necessary: once to reduce spindly winter growth by half or more before plants are set out for the summer—less if the herb has been pinched back during the winter; again, but more moderately, in early November as daylight wanes (this is a good time, too, to dry the late summer's growth of leaves).

Sooner or later tender potted herbs, which are shrubs in their native lands, will outgrow the confines of a container. This is the time to start new, small plants from cuttings. Sometimes I do this in spring but more often during August, when sturdy (as opposed to winter-spindly) new shoots are available.

Brewing

Summer is the time for cold teas made from the fruity tropicals, fragrant drinks so much more refreshing than syrupy soft drinks. Nothing could be easier; it is not even necessary to brew the herbs first. Pick a handful of each of lemon verbena, pineapple and/or fruit sage, a sheaf of spearmint, some leaves of lemon balm or anise-hyssop, perhaps a sprig of lemon or cinnamon basil. Put the works into a pitcher with a cup or two of water, then crush and macerate the leaves with the back of a wooden spoon or the end of a wire whisk. Add the juice of a lemon, fill the pitcher with water (sparkling water is a good variation), sweeten to taste—if using honey, dissolve it first in a little of the tea before adding to the pitcher—then let it stand out of the refrigerator for at least half an hour. Strain into glasses over ice, and garnish with borage flowers or a few leaves of the herb.

This recipe can be varied by crushing some strawberries or raspberries with the herbs or by using pineapple or orange juice (omit the lemon juice) in place of water. Keep in mind that the less elaborate the mixture, the more evident the herbal tastes will be.

A word about brewing the hot herb teas: "doesn't taste like anything" or "too strong" are frequent reactions. The good-tasting middle ground between insipid and medicinal can be found only by trial and error and, in fact, varies from herb to herb and taste to taste. Be guided by the scent and flavor of the herbs themselves in determining the amounts to brew and the duration of steeping: mild leaves of lemon balm, spearmint and anise-hyssop, for example, are used alone or blended in larger quantities as the predominant flavors, while stronger or more bitter flavors—a leaf or two of sage or a bit of rosemary—will add body and complexity to a blend. Most herb teas are steeped longer than black tea—5 to 10 minutes on average—but taste to be sure. It is possible to almost fill a teapot with fresh herbs and still brew a delicious tea that is not overpowering; just use proportionately fewer dried herbs. One teaspoon per cup is about right.

Each year, a neighbor, Margot Barnard, patiently gathers from her garden and the wild the 20 or so ingredients that make up her own tea blend. "This is the only herb tea my husband will drink," she says. "He doesn't even want his morning coffee anymore." I can attest that the tea is delicious, and given the extraordinary list of ingredients, it must be a potent health-promoting drink.

"It's not difficult to get the herbs together," says Margot, although "they are not all ready at once. I dry little batches of this and that all summer and blend them in the fall."

Margot's Tea Blend

2 parts each of raspberry leaves and red clover flowers, 1 part each of strawberry leaves, St. John's wort flowers, crushed rose hips, common yarrow leaves and

flowers, garden sage, horsetail leaves, black currant leaves, lemon balm, bearberry leaves, twitch grass roots, common plantain leaves, common or lemon thyme and dried apple peel, ½ part of bergamot leaves, ¼ part each of oregano leaves, violet flowers, rose petals, chamomile, mullein and calendula flowers.

Storage

The foregoing herbs alone or in varying combinations fill a teapot from day to day during the growing season. All are easy to dry for winter use: hang bundles of three or four branches (any more and drying is uneven due to bulk) anywhere out of sun where the air circulates freely. Attic rafters or a garden shed will be fine if there is ventilation. I hang bunches from a dowel suspended over the wood stove; the dry rising heat crisps them in short order. When the leaves are crackling-dry, strip them onto a sheet of newspaper, pick out bits of twigs, and funnel the herbs into jars or any containers that can be closed tightly. Store clear glass jars out of light, opaque containers anywhere. Screen drying (as described for chamomile flowers and rose hips) works for leafy herbs if fresh leaves are plucked from stems and laid in a single layer on the screen; if the screen is propped on clay pots that sit directly on the surface of a gently radiating wood stove or over a hot-air vent or register, drying is swift. Oven drying (the oven turned to its lowest setting, the oven door slightly ajar) has its proponents, but I cannot speak from experience.

I wonder if herbal teas—I'll avoid the cumbersome but more accurate term tisane—will ever catch on as a day-to-day drink in the manner of coffee and black or green tea. Probably not, yet because they soothe without sedating and refresh without the nerve-jangling effects of drinks with caffeine, herb teas are gaining popularity. Any restaurant worth its sea salt and demerara sugar now lists, in addition to black tea flavored with everything from strawberries to almonds, alternative teas—at the very least, chamomile, mint and rose hip. Ironically, this narrow range may be the reason that some people turn up their noses at herb teas in general and opt for yet another cappuccino. To my taste, the best herb teas, like the best regular teas, are blends. Unlike "real" teas, however, some of the best herbal drinks are made with fresh ingredients. Teas composed of garden-grown herbs are as varied as the imagination; a little experimental brewing and sipping are sure to result in a special blend or two. 🌿

Rue Herb Grace
Ruta graveolens

76

MEXICAN MARIGOLD MINT

Lucinda Hutson

Tagetes lucida (T. florida)
Compositae

Common Names: Mexican marigold mint, mint marigold, Texas tarragon, sweet marigold, cloud plant; *yerbanís, hierba anís, coronilla, pericón, hierba de las nubes* (Mexico); winter tarragon (England)

Characteristics: glossy lance-shaped leaves, finely serrated; strong anise scent; brilliant golden marigoldlike flowers in fall; perennial

Conditions: loose, well-drained soil; full sun

Size: 1½-2½ feet tall

Propagation: reseeds in late fall; roots in water; or plant seeds in flats (germinate in a few days) approximately 6 weeks before planting, and set out in early spring; plant 1 foot or more apart; 1-2 plants per garden suggested

Fertilizer: none required

Pests: some spider mite damage possible during hot months; spittlebugs, which may burrow in emerging leaves during high humidity, should be picked off

Companions: none noted

Lucinda Hutson lives and gardens in Austin, Texas, where she grows more than 200 kinds of herbs. She has taught cooking for 10 years and specializes in food of the Southwest. She is the author of The Herb Garden Cookbook.

Photos by Elvin McDonald

Tagetes lucida, *Mexican marigold mint, has lance-shaped leaves that release a sweet anise scent when bruised. The small yellow flowers look like miniature marigolds.*

Today I can look back with humor on some of the trials and errors I have experienced in herb gardening. Once, while passing a deserted herb plot at our local community gardens, I noticed a plant that I could not identify. Picking off a few of the lance-shaped leaves and bruising them gently released a sharp but pleasant sweet anise scent. I thought I had found French tarragon! (I had never seen it growing and was accustomed to tasting it only in its dried form.) "What a find!" I thought, carefully uprooting a small clump to transplant to my own garden. And so for a few months, I happily grew my "Texas tarragon."

One day, however, a fellow herbalist informed me that my cherished plant was not tarragon, but a somewhat similar herb commonly called Mexican marigold mint. Tarragon (an artemisia) has difficulty tolerating our hot and dry summers; in fact, it requires a cold winter during its dormancy to produce healthy spring growth. Because of this, and because tarragon does not set seed and must be propagated by cuttings, it is difficult to grow in the Southwest.

On the other hand, Mexican marigold mint flourishes in our region and can even be weedlike if not kept in check. And this plant offers an extra bonus: throughout October and November, it prolifically produces marigoldlike flowers to grace the garden. (In cases of drought, it also may try to flower in the summer to preserve the species). You can make a breathtaking bouquet by combining Mexican marigold mint's brilliant golden flowers with scarlet spikes of pineapple sage and violet-colored blossoms of Mexican sage (*Salvia leucantha*). The flowers of marigold mint also make attractive edible garnishes, and the petals may be sprinkled on salads or pasta dishes and used in vinegars and potpourris. I love to adorn the turkey platter at Thanksgiving with them.

The leaves also offer exciting culinary possibilities. Although French chefs would scoff at Mexican marigold mint replacing their beloved tarragon, I find it the best available substitute. *Estragon*, the French word for tarragon, literally means "little dragon," and there is indeed an assertive and fiery taste to tarragon that Mexican marigold mint lacks. And Mexican marigold mint's anise flavor is definitely more pronounced. But use Mexican marigold mint as you would tarragon; in fact, it gives tarragon some competition as a flavoring herb for vinegar. Vinaigrettes made with it enliven mixed spring greens and chicken, tuna or shellfish salads. (Toss about a tablespoon of the chopped fresh herb into the salad as well.)

Sauces, from the classic French *béarnaise* to homemade mayonnaise, take on a new flair when marigold mint replaces tarragon. A tablespoon of the freshly chopped herb added to a melting stick of butter with minced garlic gives steamed artichoke leaves a tasty dunk. It makes a fabulous herbal butter blended with orange zest and minced green onions and tastes delicious tossed with pasta in a creamy tomato sauce. It enhances dips for vegetables, and the sprigs make an attractive garnish.

Grilled Catfish with Smoked Peppers and Mexican Marigold Mint

Celebrated Southwestern chef Stephan Pyles of Routh Street Cafe in Dallas, well known for his magic at the grill, created this special recipe.

½ *red bell pepper, seeded and deribbed*
½ *yellow bell pepper, seeded and deribbed*
¼ *cup white wine vinegar*
1 shallot, finely diced
1 clove garlic, finely diced
8 ounces (1 cup) butter, room temperature
*1 tablespoon finely chopped fresh marigold
   mint leaves*
4 6-8 ounce catfish fillets
1 tablespoon oil or clarified butter
Salt to taste

To Prepare Peppers and Smoker

Soak 6-8 chunks of aromatic wood (such as almond, hickory, cherry, apple or orange) in water for 20 minutes. Build fire in smoker with hardwood charcoal briquettes and electric starter. (Avoid chemical starters, as they impart unpleasant flavors to the smoke.) When briquettes are still glowing but somewhat gray (about 20 minutes after starting fire), add soaked wood chunks. Let burn for 5 minutes.

Place peppers on grill over water pan and cover with top of smoker. Smoke peppers for 20-30 minutes. Remove from smoker and roast in preheated 400-degree oven for 10-15 minutes. Peel peppers and chop. Set aside.

To Make Sauce

Place vinegar, wine, shallot and garlic in a medium-size saucepan. Over high heat reduce liquid to 2 tablespoons. Over medium-low heat, begin whisking in butter, a piece at a time, until all butter is incorporated. Remove from heat.

Add chopped peppers and marigold mint. Season with salt and keep warm in pan set over barely simmering water while grilling catfish.

Salt catfish fillets to taste, and grill 3-4 minutes per side, basting with oil or butter. When fillets are done, place each on a plate and cover generously with sauce. Serves 4.

NOTE: Garnish with marigold mint sprigs and/or flowers.

Mexican Marigold Mint Butter

1-2 green onions with tops, or 1 medium
shallot, finely chopped
2-3 tablespoons finely chopped Mexican
marigold mint leaves (some of the golden
petals may be used as well)
½ teaspoon orange zest (optional)
2-3 teaspoons fresh orange juice or white
wine or dry vermouth
1-2 tablespoons chopped pecans or more
(optional)
Salt and white pepper to taste
¼-½ teaspoon dried mustard (optional)
¼ pound (1 stick) unsalted butter, softened

This tasty butter complements fish and fowl, grilled or baked, and is especially good with quail. Try it with steamed sweet potatoes or carrots; use it in stuffings and sauces. Garlic may be substituted for green onions.

Texas Tarragon (Mexican Marigold Mint) Vinegar

Fill jar ½ full of fresh Mexican marigold mint. (I generally remove the leaves from the stems so the vinegar won't taste too strong or become dark.) Cover with heated white wine or apple cider vinegar. After straining,

I often add small bouquets of marigold mint's colorful golden flowers to each bottle. This vinegar's strong, aniselike aroma greatly enhances vegetables and soups. I like to use it in pickling beets and in making a zesty vinaigrette with Dijon mustard and honey. It makes a wonderful marinade when oil and garlic are added for wild game, chicken and pork. Delicious with seafood salads and in homemade mayonnaise.

Because this herb grows so plentifully in my garden, I have devised innumerable ways to use it. I add a tablespoon of whole, fresh leaves to a quart jar of pickled beets, and a few teaspoons of minced leaves to crunchy carrots sautéed in butter. A simple entrée can be prepared by stuffing minced garlic and marigold mint leaves under the skin of chicken before baking or grilling it.

Others also extol the versatility of this flavorful herb. Mexican marigold mint has recently become the darling of renowned Southwestern chefs such as Stephan Pyles (Routh Street Cafe in Dallas), who partners it with catfish and smoked tomatoes. Anne Greer (author of several Southwestern cuisine books) uses it with pecans to make a unique pesto. Robert Del Grande (Cafe Annie in Houston), uses the flowers in his spectacular salads and various fish dishes. And the Mozzarella Company in Dallas adds it to *caciotta* cheese, giving it a uniquely delicious flavor.

Mexican marigold mint makes a pleasant flavoring for hot and cold beverages alike. As a tea, it is slightly sweet and refreshing. I also add it to fruit punches and sangria. Hot mulled apple cider warmly welcomes guests in the fall, filling the house with its spicy redolence. As marigold mint is at its peak at this time, I add a few large sprigs to the simmering cider and garnish each mug with a sprig of the cheerful golden flowers, evoking enthusiastic comments.

Germans traditionally drink May wine to celebrate winter's passing into spring, serving it from ornate crystal punch bowls adorned with garlands of the season's fresh-

Photo by Elvin McDonald

Tarragon (an artemisia) has difficulty tolerating the hot dry summers of the South and it also needs a cold winter during its dormancy to produce healthy spring growth. Tarragon can be substituted for Mexican mint in any of the recipes.

est flowers and strawberries. May wine is customarily flavored with sweet woodruff, an herb with a woodsy nutmeg flavor that simply cannot abide the heat of the Southwest. Consequently, I have adapted May wine to our part of the country by replacing sweet woodruff with marigold mint and calling it Mexican May wine. This makes a festive drink to serve on the Mexican holiday often celebrated in the Southwest, *Cinco de Mayo.* Remember to decorate the base of the serving bowl with long stems of marigold mint and the garden's finest flowers (float them as well) and fruits.

Fortunately, Mexican marigold mint is now available from several seed catalogs, but unless you plan to grow it for an ornamental border, I recommend buying one or two plants the first year. Believe me, by the following year it will have readily reseeded! Or take a few cuttings from a friend, as they root in water. Plants should be spaced about one-and-one-half feet apart because they will grow a few feet wide and approximately two feet tall with long, spindly branches abundantly covered with finely serrated lanceolate leaves. A well-drained soil and plenty of sunshine are necessary to produce the brilliant golden flowers.

Although I always cook with this herb in its fresh form, I also hang large bunches of it to dry in a well-ventilated room and then store it in jars to use as a tea or as a spicy and fragrant addition to potpourri. Actually, some chefs prefer it in its dried form, as its taste is more mellow. One note of caution: some find marigold mint's flavor overpowering, especially those who dislike the taste of anise; therefore, you may want to use it judiciously at first. Fortunately, I find its perky flavor and versatility an attribute. ♣

Mustard and Marigold Mint Chicken

In this dish, Mexican marigold mint gives tarragon some competition! Served warm or cold, this chicken makes lively picnic fare when sliced into medallions and served on baguette slices spread with honey-mustard. Garnish with fresh sprigs of marigold mint.

4 boneless chicken breasts, split, with skin
Salt and freshly ground pepper to taste
3 green onions, with tops
2-3 cloves garlic, minced
2-3 tablespoons chopped fresh marigold mint
3 tablespoons Dijon mustard
2 teaspoons honey
2 tablespoons butter, softened
1 tablespoon dry vermouth or white wine

Slightly flatten breasts and trim excess fat. Sprinkle with salt and pepper. Set aside.

Combine the remaining ingredients to make a thick paste. Place approximately 1½ tablespoons of the paste on each breast (skin-side down), and roll up tightly from end to end, starting with wider end. Place seam-side down on a lightly oiled baking dish, and dot breasts with any remaining herb mixture. Bake in preheated 350-degree oven for about 30 minutes. Serves 4.

NOTE: Fresh tarragon or dill may be substituted for Mexican marigold mint. Sliced into medallions, chicken may be served warm or cold in salads with crisp greens. Allow 3-4 slices per salad and dress with marigold mint vinaigrette.

Shared Lessons From Southern Gardens

Linda Askey Weathers

Gardening brings out the best in each of us. Sharing seems to be our trademark, whether it's unloading summer's excess basil or gingerly dividing the sweet woodruff. Information is as precious as the plants, for without it, the little gifts you take home may not survive. So off you go, with a fragile division in hand and your head full of advice.

Growing herbs in the Southeast has always depended on shared experience. Published expertise from northern states or from countries across the Atlantic has not considered the hot days, warm nights, and humid air that are the challenge for both people and plants in the South.

Pineapple sage, Salvia elegans, *adds a decorative element to BBG's Fragrance Garden. It seems to tolerate the harsh summers and mild winters of the South.*

Rosemary will survive the hot summers of Miami Beach, Florida. In fact, it grew to five to six feet in diameter and had to be cut back.

Linda Askey Weathers grows herbs, perennials and vegetables in her Birmingham, Alabama, garden. She is Associate Garden Editor for Southern Living *magazine and an active member of the Garden Writers of America.*

Photos by Elvin McDonald

But even within the Southeast, conditions can vary greatly. The mountainous regions are probably most like the texts, with their own microclimates to be explored. The foothills and Piedmont require an appreciation for shade on the part of people and plants alike. Florida presents the most drastic change of all where seasons are reversed.

No one gardener can know the demands of these areas as well as the people who garden there, so I have talked with three southern gardeners, who have also lived in other areas of the country. This puts them in a unique position to know what is different about growing herbs in the South. And in typical fashion, they have generously shared their experience.

Calera McHenry, Cullman, Alabama

"Full sun in the South is different from full sun in the North. So many times people can grow plants very successfully, in fact better, in partial shade than in full sun. Growing in filtered light is ideal for plants that are tender and wilt readily. Borage looks pretty in partial shade, and it keeps flowering and re-seeding. I can grow lovage quite successfully under pine trees. So many plants do very well in partial shade. These can be anything from comfrey to costmary to sweet marjoram. Golden creeping marjoram does much better in shade than sun. The golden color browns off during the heat of summer and looks parched. If you grow it in partial shade, it's much happier.

"Our temperatures with high humidity are not conducive to good growth. For instance, thymes have problems with a mold that is caused by high humidity and makes them look very unattractive. I suggest mulching for lavenders, thymes and other plants that touch the soil. I heartily recommend some type of mulch on top of the ground to conserve moisture and make it look more attractive. If the plant is touching the ground, add a layer of sand around the plant. The sand lets water get on through without staying wet all the time, whereas bark mulch holds the moisture. A half-inch of white builders' sand is ideal."

You might think that milder winters would compensate for the harsh summer conditions. And that is true for many tender perennials. Calera explains, "I don't always manage to bring them through winter, but I want my plants to stand on their own as much as possible. We are all very busy people and we don't have time to protect all these different plants with different requirements. Therefore we need to know which ones may not make it. If they don't, we'll buy another plant. That's how I feel about *Lavandula*, sweet lavender. It grows so quickly. However, my Mexican sage and pineapple sage comes back here, as it did in Georgia. Many people dig it up before it comes back from the root system. If I put a spading fork in there and feel resistance, I leave it alone and let it come back."

Cold temperatures are necessary for some plants. "I've never had any trouble with French tarragon. I've lived in New York, Colorado, Arizona, North Carolina, Texas and New Mexico, and grown it successfully in each state. It has to have a dormant period. It will not go dormant in a warm place and revive to a healthy, growing plant. You'll get a spindly plant. My brother lives in Naples, Florida. He could not get his plant to make it; it was too warm."

For improved winter hardiness, Calera recommends protection from the wind, not cutting back so severely that you induce new growth, and not fertilizing too late in the season. "I like to apply bone meal rather than a high nitrogen fertilizer. *Lavandula angustifolia* and *L. latifolia* are growing during the winter months. Not a great deal, but when the temperatures are 50 degrees F, they are not completely dormant. Therefore they still need some nutrients. I also apply granular limestone. On a plant that is two-feet high, apply a quarter cup of each around the drip line of the plant."

Tip: "I add tarragon and *Tagetes lucida* (sweet-scented marigold) to meat dishes, mayonnaise and Bearnaise sauce, and they are great with fruits or as marinades for fruit compotes. Leave them in there until the flavor melds. It's very nice."

Susan Tulloch, Miami Beach, Florida

"Our location in South Florida is really subtropical. There are two seasons. The season when you grow culinary herbs such as thyme and basil starts around October. Then another season starts in April or May. That's when you grow the tropicals like lemon grass and Mexican oregano.

Rosemary
Rosmarinus officinalis

"You are usually better off treating most herbs as annuals, because they fry in the summer. Our seasons are reversed, but we also have a rainy season and a dry season. Summer is the rainy season. We start getting some rain in April and May. Then in summer it rains almost every day. So anything that doesn't like a lot of water will get rained out.

"Rosemary will make it through the summer. I lived in upstate New York for a long time and struggled with it every year. Here in Miami it grew to five to six feet in diameter, and I had to cut it back.

"Thai basil, dill and cilantro will also make it through summer. I never plant those anymore—they just reseed.

"Winter is the dry season when you have to water. We can go three months without a drop of rain—just one beautiful day after another.

"The artemisia genus is difficult. I find that tarragon, southernwood and 'Silver King' don't perform well. You can grow them in winter, but just for a few months before it gets hot. I do grow *Artemisia annua*. I love the smell of it, and it reseeds as well.

"I live on one of the islands between Miami and Miami Beach and our soil is really sandy. Just south of me, Coral Gables and environs are all coral rock. At Fairchild Tropical Garden planting holes were blasted. Now holes are made by picking with an axe. Raised beds can be made and soil added as another solution. Where there is soil, it's very alkaline. It's fine for herbs as far as pH, but it's very nutrient deficient. With the heavy rains and the sunshine, you lose a tremendous amount of nutrients from the soil, so you have to fertilize.

"If you're not using organic sources, the best thing to do is use Osmocote a couple of times during the season. Dig it in when you plant and it will last two to three months. You can apply again in January.

"I make compost and side dress every few weeks. I also apply seaweed and fish emulsion."

Susan also recommends using generous amounts of sphagnum peat moss or other organic matter when you first prepare your soil. By adding compost regularly, she replenishes the soil each year.

Tip: "I make pincushions from dried rosemary leaves. It's so humid down here in the summertime that everything rusts, including your sewing needles. It seems to me that the oils in the rosemary pincushion keep the needles from rusting as quickly as they do normally."

Ruth Wrensch, Tryon, North Carolina

"My training is in botany and chemistry, which I apply to gardening. I compare the native habitat of an herb to where I want to grow it. If you think of many herbs coming from the Mediterranean area and compare that climate to the southeastern United States, you find some notable differences.

"I have photographs of herbs growing in their native habitats. You see a rosemary growing on a hillock in a very arid climate on meager, rocky, calcareous soil. You can grow it in the Southeast if you apply yourself and give the plant what it wants. I would plant it on a hillock where the air can circulate around it and so the fungus infections will be discouraged. I'd provide an alkaline soil, supplemented with oyster shells. On the surface they will reflect back light, preventing the germination of spores.

"There are many herbs that, even though they come from a certain habitat and certain climate, will adapt.

"My garden is divided according to native habitats. We have a garden that is planted as a Mediterranean landscape. Other gardens include herbs from south of the border (Argentina, Chile and Mexico) and native American herbs.

"In this warm climate substitute *Tagetes lucida* for tarragon. Tarragon comes from Siberia where it gets to be 20 below zero F. It does well because it gets that nice cold rest period. Here it is always struggling, and it never develops a good root system.

"*Tagetes lucida* is similar in flavor to tarragon. It has that aniselike, licorice flavor, but it is slightly different. For instance, I don't think it is as lasting as tarragon in vinegar or when dried. If you're making tarragon chicken, use more. However, on salads, as chopped greens, and dressed with vinegar, it is delicious.

"If I compared it to tarragon grown in a colder climate, then I think there would be a greater difference. I originally came from Wisconsin and tarragon was the first thing that came up. By mid-April it's three feet high and you're cutting it down. In two-and-a-half weeks it's back up again. It's not handsome, but it's the aristocrat in the kitchen.

"You can help it along here by encouraging that early growth in the spring. As soon as it's about six or eight inches high, cut it back and preserve that first crop. Give it fertilizer. And then you will get another crop, but never the abundance that you get in the North. It will grow eight to twelve inches high and the patch will increase. Then it will limp along through the heat.

"I live on a thermal belt in the foothills of the Blue Ridge mountains. I can grow any number of subtropical plants here in protected spots. The house protects the garden from north and west winds.

"Even within the Southeast, you have to consider separate areas, depending upon the elevation. Just 18 miles away in Henderson County, they can grow tarragon much better than I can. They grow wonderful angelica, and their lovage will grow six to eight feet tall like it does in the Midwest. But they have more trouble with the freezing out of some plants. This is the Southeast."

Tip: "I like to make little wreaths of sweet woodruff that fit over candlesticks to catch the drips. As the candle burns and the heat gets down lower, the oil is emitted from the sweet woodruff, providing fragrance." ❧

Civilized Solutions
to the Hurried Meal

Ann Lovejoy

Today's supermarkets offer squid and satsumas, jicama and juniper berries, cilantro and sorrel. *Eight Items Or Less** shows the busy cook how to use these exotic, fresh ingredients—previously available only in specialty outlets—to create fine meals with flair.

Two hundred entrees featuring unusual and seasonal foods help you break out of cooking routines. For each recipe the shopping list stays short and the preparation time minimal. With the convenience of one-stop

Large leaves of basil can be stuffed and served as hors d'oeuvres. Here tabouleh salad was used. The ties are garlic chives.

Chopped basil adds a wonderful touch to many dishes, especially those containing tomatoes. The recipe on page 89 for sirloin tip and pan-fried tomatoes contains fresh basil.

shopping, hurried mealtimes can become culinary discoveries.

Cooking with *Eight Items Or Less* will speed you from the supermarket express lane to a delicious meal—whether a bite for two or a banquet for ten. Thanks to these streamlined, sophisticated recipes, newly discovered foods such as star fruit, tiny pumpkins, blue corn tortillas and enoki mushrooms will

Eight Items or Less, by Ann Lovejoy, is published by Sasquatch Books in Seattle, Washington.

become kitchen staples, to give everyday meals the panache of party food.

Cilantro Pesto Pizza

(Serves up to 4)

This nontraditional pizza has a green sauce hot with chiles and cilantro. The zesty pesto is also wonderful on pork, chicken or turkey; try adding a bit of coriander, cumin and even caraway—many variations are delightful. Pizza crusts, fresh from the bakery or frozen, are available in most supermarkets. Keep a couple in the freezer for quick and different dinners like this one. Use any nuts you prefer—almonds, walnuts, pine nuts—with the possible exception of peanuts. Have a salad of chunky summer vegetables dressed with yogurt and herbs, and drink a glass of Chianti or beer.

1 9-inch pizza crust or sourdough baguette
2 tablespoons olive oil
2 bunches fresh cilantro, trimmed and
  chopped
2 fresh chiles (pasillas, hot wax, or any),
  seeded and chopped
2 cloves garlic, chopped
¼ cup pine nuts, almonds or walnuts,
  coarsely chopped
2 ounces grated parmesan cheese
8 ounces mozzarella cheese, sliced or grated

Preheat oven to 425 degrees. Place crust on a baking sheet and brush with oil. Put cilantro in blender or food processor with chiles, garlic, nuts, 2 to 3 tablespoons parmesan and 2 to 3 tablespoons oil, buzz to blend, adding more oil if needed to produce a thick paste. Scrape pesto out of blender (a narrow rubber spatula works very well), pour, and spread evenly over crust. Sprinkle on remaining parmesan. Spread mozzarella over top; the greater amount will please fans of very cheesy pizza. Bake for 15 to 20 minutes until golden brown and bubbly. Cut in pieces with scissors or pizza wheel. Serve at once.

Cured and Smoked Meats

Smoked Turkey Salad in Poppy Seed Dressing

Smoked turkey is frequently found in the supermarket beside the Canadian bacon, the hard sausages, and other specialty meats. For the best flavor, choose a brand that is naturally smoked rather than one slathered with liquid smoke and pumped full of chemicals. Not only will it smell and taste better, the meat will be more tender as well. Here, smoked turkey chunks, pink grapefruit sections and watercress meet in a sage-scented vinaigrette that is crunchy with pine nuts and grainy with poppy seeds. You can always substitute romaine or endive for the watercress, or use mixed greens with some shreds of arugula and green onion. A crusty baguette and a glass of dry chardonnay are all you need on the side.

2 bunches fresh watercress, chopped
8 ounces smoked turkey, cut into chunks
1 small pink grapefruit, peeled and
  sectioned
2 tablespoons vinaigrette
1 teaspoon minced fresh sage or
  ½ teaspoon dried
2 tablespoons pine nuts, toasted
2 tablespoons poppy seeds

Line a salad bowl with watercress. Gently toss together turkey and grapefruit and mound on watercress. Blend vinaigrette, sage, pine nuts and poppy seeds; pour over salad, toss and serve.

Lamb and Beans

Thick lamb medallions broil, grill or pan-sauté in minutes and need very little help to make them delectable (any of these cooking techniques may be used with the following sauce). Properly cooked lamb, by any method, is fork-tender, pink and generously juicy when sliced. Overcooked lamb is gray, tough, and nasty; no sauce can really help, so keep your eye on the cooking time. Fresh herbs make a big difference here, especially the savory, though it retains flavor fairly well when dried. Summer savory is the classic companion for fresh beans, just as winter savory (or dried summer savory) goes into the winter bean pot. This entrée invites a simple rice and cilantro pilaf, a cucumber, orange, and onion salad with an herbed vinaigrette, and a glass of chiaretto or a sturdy ale.

2 to 4 lamb medallions (8 to 12 ounces total)
2 teaspoons butter
½ teaspoon black peppercorns, cracked
1 onion, cut into thin half-moon slices
4 ounces snap beans, thinly sliced on
  the diagonal
3 tomatoes, cut into wedges
1 teaspoon chopped fresh lemon thyme
1 teaspoon chopped fresh savory (reserve
  a few leaves for garnish)

Rinse lamb, pat dry. Rub lightly with butter, pat on cracked peppercorns. Preheat broiler. In a frying pan, heat remaining butter over medium heat. Add onion, beans, tomatoes and herbs; stir to coat and cook for 5 minutes. Mash tomatoes with a fork, and reduce heat to warm. While vegetables are cooking, broil lamb for 4 to 6 minutes per side. To serve, spoon sauce onto plates, set lamb medallions on top and garnish with a sprig or 2 of savory.

Rabbit

Hunter's Rabbit

Rabbit has a stronger flavor than chicken, though not by much, and farm-raised animals have none of the gamier overtones often found in wild rabbits. You can use nearly any chicken recipe with rabbit, allowing a bit more cooking time, and conversely, any of these rabbit recipes can be made with chicken or game hens. This one uses the herbs of the Mediterranean fields in a combination favored by hunters, who might gather the herbs as they wandered home, rabbit in the bag. Sometimes garlic tips are sold in the markets along with Chinese mustard greens. If you garden at home, you can snip the shoots of the emerging garlic without hurting the plants one bit. Garlic chives or a clove or two of garlic make a very acceptable substitute. Sweet potatoes and parsnips may be parboiled and grilled along with the rabbit, or serve up new potatoes, infant peas and tiny fingerling beans in dill and chive butter. Warm rolls for sopping up the satiny sauce will be welcome, as will a glass of sprightly weissbier or a dry blush wine.

1 rabbit, cut up by butcher
2 tablespoons olive oil
½ lemon, juiced
2 teaspoons chopped fresh sage
½ teaspoon black peppercorns, cracked
1 bulb Florence fennel with leaves, thinly
  sliced
1 bunch garlic tips, chopped (2 to 3 table-
  spoons)
2 tablespoons balsamic vinegar

Rinse rabbit, pat dry. In a frying pan, blend oil, lemon juice, sage, peppercorns and 1 tablespoon fennel leaves over medium heat. Warm combination for 3 to 5 minutes, then lightly brush it on rabbit pieces. Grill rabbit for 10 to 12 minutes on a side, turning several times. Add fennel, garlic tips and vinegar to remaining oil mixture and simmer for 5 to 7 minutes over medium heat, until fennel is tender-crisp. Serve each portion of rabbit with several spoonsful of sauce.

Green Eggs and Ham

A foamy green sauce that tastes of spring envelops strips of lean ham and hard-cooked eggs. This pretty mixture of greens, herbs and walnuts is as good with chicken or fish as in salads like this one. Rinse, but don't spin-dry the greens; just shake them gently, for they cook in the steam from water that clings to their leaves. Pass a plate of thin watercress sandwiches, a basket of fruit and a bottle of lemony weissbier, dry Orvieto or hard cider.

1 bunch fresh spinach, rinsed and trimmed
1 bunch fresh sorrel, rinsed and trimmed
4 ounces lean ham, sliced into thin strips

3 hard-boiled eggs, quartered
2 tablespoons olive oil
1 bunch fresh watercress, rinsed and
   trimmed
1 small bunch fresh chives, rinsed and
   chopped
¼ cup walnuts, toasted

Arrange a few leaves of spinach and sorrel on each plate; top with ham and eggs. In a small heavy saucepan, heat 1 teaspoon oil over medium heat. Add remaining spinach and sorrel, watercress and chives. Cover pan and cook over medium heat for 5 to 6 minutes, shaking pan several times. Greens should be limp but still bright green. Put greens in blender or food processor with remaining oil and half the walnuts, adding 1 to 2 table-

Wonderful marinades can be made using herbs—especially for basting on the backyard barbeque. See the recipe for hunter's rabbit on page 87.

Photo by Elvin McDonald

Basil is the basis for the wonderful pesto being sampled here. Other herbs can be the basis of pesto as well. See the recipe for cilantro pesto pizza on page 86.

spoons water as needed to make a smooth sauce. Pour over salads, top with remaining walnuts and serve at once.

Seafood

Sorrel Soup with Shrimp and Bacon

In the Northwest and other mild-winter areas, sorrel has two seasons, spring and fall. The epicurean French have elevated this humble meadow weed to the haute cuisine, taming the puckering, astringent quality of wild sorrel to a tingling, piquant sourness. In the best strains, young sorrel is mild enough to eat raw, snipped into spring salads. Here, sorrel's tartness is deliciously offset by crumbled bacon and sweet shrimp in a rich soup that is as bright and green as spring itself. Like spinach, sorrel cooks down a great deal, so although four bunches seems like a

Photo by Inger Skaarup

lot, it ends up being a modest amount. A salad of young lettuce and mustard greens dressed with a curried vinaigrette, hot rolls, a piece of aged cheese and a glass of stout make this a delightful meal to enjoy indoors or out.

1 tablespoon butter
4 bunches (4 cups) sorrel, rinsed and
*   trimmed*
3 cups milk
2 strips bacon
6 ounces shrimp, cooked
2 tablespoons sour cream
1 green onion, sliced into thin circles

In a heavy saucepan, melt half the butter over low heat. Add damp sorrel; cover and cook slowly until tender and limp, about 12 to 15 minutes. While sorrel is cooking, scald milk. In a frying pan, cook bacon over medium heat; drain off grease. When sorrel is done, add 1 cup scalded milk to saucepan (it will curdle), stirring well. Put in a blender or food processor and buzz until smooth. Return to saucepan, add remaining milk, butter, shrimp and sour cream; heat until butter melts. Ladle into bowls, garnish with green onions and crumbled bacon. Serve at once.

Beef and Lamb

Sirloin Tip with Pan-fried Tomatoes

Red meat has been unfashionable for some time, but that never stopped people from buying it. It did, however, prompt meat department managers to stock leaner cuts in smaller portions, and both of these moves have been well received. A good steak needs very little help, but it must be acknowledged that leaner cuts, though nutritionally sounder, are less flavorful than well-marbled ones, for the fat carries much of the flavor. Slimmed-down cuts call for more exciting treatments—rich, spicy or savory ones that emphasize rather than mask the flavor of the meat. Add a spinach, snow pea and walnut salad, toss it with a mustardy vinaigrette and pass around a bottle of Chianti Classico.

12 ounces thick-cut sirloin tip steak
½ teaspoon freshly ground black pepper
1 tablespoon butter
2 tomatoes, halved
1 tablespoon minced fresh basil
1 tablespoon minced fresh chives
¼ cup crème fraiche or sour cream

Start coals or preheat broiler. Rinse steak, pat dry. Pat pepper onto both sides of steak. In a heavy frying pan, melt butter over medium heat until foamy. Add tomatoes, cut-side down, and herbs. Prick tomatoes several times with a knife tip. Cook tomatoes slowly for 10 minutes, turn and cook for another 10 minutes. Start cooking steak, allowing 6 to 8 minutes per side. When steak is turned to second side, swirl crème fraîche into sauce, but do not break up tomatoes. To serve, cut steak in 2 portions, set each on a plate with 2 tomato halves, and pour sauce around each serving. Garnish with a few herb leaves. ❧

Nice large leaves of basil have been washed and are ready for stuffing. With a bit of imagination, a host of innovative stuffings can be prepared.

To really showcase the flavor of herbs try. . .

DESSERT FROM
THE HERB GARDEN

Ron Zimmerman

It is now four years since we pounded the last nail, plastered the walls, daubed and dry brushed on the three colors of paint, hung the great old mirror, reupholstered the chairs, set out glazed mustard crocks of herbs and flowers and welcomed the first small group of diners to our little restaurant on our farm in Fall City, Washington.

The dining room at The Herbfarm was to have been an experiment, a sideline, an interlude on the way to other now-forgotten things. We would combine the local foods of the Northwest with fresh herbs from our farm's gardens, serve it all up in a progression of six courses, dust off our hands, say "Thank you" and . . .

Four years have passed. I watch as a bejeweled herbal punch is poured, flashing in the sunlight. Outside a jaunty rooster crows, turtle doves are cooing from their rustic cote, and we are enveloped by the perfume of our 16 herb gardens as we chop, dice, stir, baste and taste, taste, taste—for it is but moments before we greet today's diners and begin to dish up yet another herbal adventure.

In these four years, herbs have drawn us deep into their magic, and their magic brings to us an unending stream of pilgrims eager to

delight in the ever-changing litany of flavors.

Who would have guessed when we began that herbally flavored desserts would become a mainstay and highlight of these meals? Surely, we knew, herbs belonged to fish, fowl, meat and vegetables. But dessert?

Yet as we've sought to introduce people to herbs, we've found that few foods offer as much opportunity to showcase a single herbal flavor as do ice creams and sorbets. Additionally, fresh herbs complement and enhance seasonal fruits and berries. They are also delightful in baked goods of all sorts.

When using herbs to create desserts at our restaurant, we find it useful to think of them by natural flavor groups. So try some of the following Herbfarm dessert recipes. When you're comfortable with these recipes, substitute herbs from the categories below to mix and match while you make your own herbal discoveries.

Basic Herbal Flavors

Pungent and savory: Rosemary, thymes, oregano, marjoram, savory, sage and some basils.

Minty: Mints, balms, some basils, monarda, perilla, costmary, hyssop, wintergreen.

Lemon: Lemon balm, lemon thyme, lemon verbena, lemon basil, lemon grass, some scented geraniums.

Floral: Roses, lavender, violets, jasmine, honeysuckle, saffron, some scented geraniums.

Ron Zimmerman is president of The Herbfarm in Fall City, Washington. The Herbfarm offers hundreds of different herb plants, display gardens, herb classes, gifts and mail-order shopping. Mr. Zimmerman is also the chef at the farm's acclaimed restaurant.

Fruity: Fruit-scented sage, pineapple sage, sweet woodruff, bergamot flowers.
Spicy: Pinks, ginger.
Menthol: California bay laurel, horehound, some thymes.
Anise: Anise, tarragon, chervil, fennel, anise-hyssop, Mexican tarragon, sweet cicely, licorice, 'Irish Lace' marigold leaves.

Seasonal Melon Balls with Honey and Fresh Sage

Serves 8

This preparation is simple and absolutely delicious. Use whatever melons are ripe as well as your choice of sage: English, tricolor, purple and pineapple all work well.

2 pounds of assorted melons: watermelon, cantaloupe, honeydew and/or musk-melon
4 tbls. honey
2 ½ tbls. fresh sage leaves, chopped fine to medium-fine
Optional: pinch of salt

Prepare melon:
With a teaspoon or melon baller, ball melon and remove seeds as necessary.

Finish, chill and serve:
Stir in honey and work well to coat the melon pieces. Add sage leaves and optional pinch of salt. Toss well.

Chill thoroughly. Serve garnished with a sage leaf.

Helpful hints
• *If the melon is not absolutely ripe and luscious, add a teaspoon of balsamic vinegar.*
• *For a change of pace, add a teaspoon of crushed peppercorn to the above recipe.*

Sorbet of Rose Geranium and Sweet Cicely

Serves 4 to 6

The rose geranium is a distant cousin of the common geranium. It was first brought to Europe by sailors who found it in southern Africa in 1634. The richly perfumed leaves are the stuff of our magic here, imbuing the ice with a lovely rose scent. Sweet cicely by contrast comes from northern Europe. It is also known as anise or giant chervil and reaches heights of three to four feet. Here the sweet cicely lends the sorbet just a hint of anise and reduces the amount of sugar needed.

1 ¾ cups water
13 tbls. sugar
12 rose geranium leaves
12 6" sweet cicely sprigs
4 tbls. lemon juice

Prepare the sugar syrup:
Combine about ¾ of the sugar with all of the water. Bring the mixture to a boil and allow to cool to room temperature.

Process the herb leaves:
Put the remaining sugar in a food processor. Add the rose geranium leaves and sweet cicely sprigs and process with the steel blade for 3 or 4 minutes.

Steep the herbal sugar:
Add the herbal purée to the cooled sugar syrup. Stir and let mixture stand for at least 1 hour.

Strain through a very fine sieve or several layers of cheesecloth. Add lemon juice to taste.

Freeze:
Freeze in an ice cream machine according to manufacturer's directions. Or pour mixture into a metal bowl and place in the freezer. Scrape down sides every hour or so until frozen (allow at least 3 to 4 hours).

Serve:
Serve in chilled glasses garnished with an edible rose geranium blossom.

Crabapple & Tarragon Sorbet

Makes 8 servings

At The Herbfarm, we have a particularly fine crabapple tree which showers us with scarlet-blushed yellow fruit that reaches its sweet-

Photo by Inger Skaarup

Many unusual and flavorful ice creams can be made using fruits and herbs. The one pictured is made from plum and garnished with mint. Lavender ice cream is featured in a recipe on this page.

tart peak in the last week of July or first week of August. When combined with fresh tarragon from the herb garden, it makes a wonderfully colored and tasty sorbet.

½ pound crabapples
5-6 tbls. sugar
1 6" sprig fresh tarragon
1-2 tsp. lemon juice
water to cover crabapples

Prepare apples:

Slice the crabapples in half lengthwise. Place in a pot and cover generously with water. Bring to a boil, reduce heat and simmer until apples are very tender. Purée apples with cooking water in a food processor fitted with the metal blade. Strain through a fine sieve.

Finish sorbet base:

Add the sugar. Taste and add more if apples are particularly sour. Place liquid in a pot, bring once again to a boil, reduce heat, add the tarragon sprig and simmer 2 to 3 minutes. Strain out tarragon. Cool and add lemon juice.

Freeze and serve:

Freeze in an ice cream machine according to the manufacturer's directions. Alternately, freeze in a metal bowl set in the freezer. Scrape down the sides from time to time (every hour or two). Break up and stir the frozen mixture well. Sorbet will be ready to serve in 3 or 4 hours.

Lavender Ice Cream

Serves 8—makes 1 quart

The smell of lavender is enough to conjure memories of other times. Here we take both the leaves and flowers of English lavender and infuse it to produce an ice cream subtly flavored and tinted with the herb of love.

2 tbls. fresh or dried lavender flowers
½ cup water
1⅓ cup half & half
2⅔ cup heavy cream
14 tbls. sugar
6 egg yolks
12 lavender leaves (top 4-inch leaf tips)

Prepare lavender flowers:

Place lavender flowers and water in a small pot. Cover with a metal bowl. Fill metal bowl with cold water and ice cubes.

Turn heat to medium. Cook gently for 10 to 15 minutes. Turn off heat. Let set ½ hour. Carefully bounce the metal bowl against the pot to shake off water on the underside. Strain flowers from water—and reserve *both*.

Infuse ice cream custard base:

In a medium pot, mix half & half, cream and sugar. Carefully bring mixture to a bare boil (you should have only small bubbles forming around the edge of the pot). Add lavender leaves as well as the flowers. Let steep for 20 minutes; then add the lavender water. Remove from heat. Strain to remove leaves and blossoms, pressing hard to extract all the flavor and color.

Thicken the custard base:

In another pot, break up the egg yolks with a fork. Slowly add the warm lavender cream a little at a time, stirring constantly. Return the mixture to the stove and thicken over medium heat until the mixture will coat the back of a spoon.

Strain the mixture through a fine strainer. Set over a cold water bath to chill down custard. Refrigerate at least one hour before freezing.

Freeze & serve:
Freeze in an ice cream machine according to the manufacturer's directions.

Serve in chilled glasses and garnish with a few lavender flowers.

Helpful hints
• *Be sure your custard base is thoroughly chilled before you freeze it in an electric ice cream machine. If it isn't, your ice cream may turn out slightly gritty. This is caused by very tiny particles of butter forming during a too-slow freezing period.*
• *If you don't have an ice cream machine, you can still make a delicious dessert. Put the custard base in a metal bowl in the freezer. Scrape down the sides every hour or so as the mixture freezes.*

'Lady Plymouth' is a rose-scented geranium that can be used in the sorbet featured on page 91. The leaves have a lovely rose scent and add magic to the recipe.

Photos by Elvin McDonald

Pictured here are an old rose and the narrow, gray-green leaves of Lavandula. *Use the leaves and flowers of lavender in the custard base of ice cream.*

Rosemary-Thyme Shortbread Cookies

Makes 2-3 doz. small cookies

These cookies are ideal with herbal ice creams. Since they are a true shortbread cookie, bake them only until they are barely colored—there is little moisture in them.

1½ cups flour
¼ cup powdered sugar
9 tbls. unsalted butter
2 tbls. fresh rosemary, chopped fine
2 tsp. fresh thyme, chopped fine
1 tbl. granulated sugar to sprinkle on top

Make dough:
Work together the sugar and butter. Add the flour, rosemary and thyme. Knead together to make a soft dough.

Carefully roll out the dough to about ⅜" thick. Cut into squares, rounds or other small shapes—leaves are nice.

Bake:
Bake on a greased cookie sheet in a moderate 350-degree oven for 15 to 20 minutes—or until the cookies are a light golden color. Do not overcook.

Sprinkle cookies with the granulated sugar. Cool and store in an airtight container.✽

Seek And Ye Shall Find

Barbara J. Barton

erbs! I'm not into herbs! My first reaction when asked to write a few
words about herbs is terror, and yet
a stroll along my gopher-ravaged perennial
border reveals that I do, in fact, grow many
herbs with great pleasure: yarrow, bee balm,
wormwood, Russian sage, lamb's ears, violets, foxgloves, lavender, rosemary, lavender
cotton, sage, mint, feverfew, woolly thyme
and more borage than I ever dreamed of
when I first put in one or two plants for the
pretty blue flowers. Not yet caught up in the
rage for herb crafts and lore, I already love a
number of plants classified as herbs because
they grow beautifully and without fuss, seem
to take less water and look wonderful over
a long period. Furthermore, most of these
plants have been ignored by the gophers who
cheerfully pull down my other treasures;
perhaps the gophers don't relish the stronger
fragrance or flavor of the herbs (deer definitely tend to avoid plants with pungent
tastes and odors).

My next reaction is to find out more about
the plants themselves, their garden interest
and how to grow them. My garden is "cottage
inspired" if the meaning of that is an air of
benign neglect or a too casual devotion to
plants of every kind; there are no cunning
brick paths or gaily painted plant labels, but
there are many treasures carried home from

plant club meetings, presented by friends or
grown from seed ordered from afar. Having
mind-gardened from catalogs and books for
years before I had garden space to try out my
ideas, I want to know *everything* about a
plant before deciding whether to fall in love
and invite it home. Being the possessor of a
huge collection of nursery and seed catalogs,
I turn not to the plethora of lovely illustrated
books on herbs but to my herb catalogs to
find the sort of information that I most want
to know.

Personally, I feel a catalog should combine
entertainment, education and seduction. My
favorite catalogs educate first, but also enter-
tain with the writer's personal experience
with and honest opinions of the plants, and
seduce not just with pretty pictures but also
with the lure of trying something new and
special. H re's where the writer has to pass
the "must- ave test": if reading the catalog
makes me reach for a pen and start marking
plants before sober good sense intervenes, it's
a really good catalog. I like catalogs which are
like personal letters from the seller to the
buyer, straight talk from a more experienced
friend; I'm also a firm believer in full dis-
closure, and want to learn the quirks and
faults of the plants as well as to hear their
praises.

As I changed from a catalog junkie into a
professional catalog maven I found other
musts. Good plant descriptions with size,
plant habit, season and color of bloom are

*Barbara Barton lives and gardens in
Sebastopol, California. Her pioneering work,*
Gardening by Mail, *is now in its third edition.*

essential. Also important is the inclusion of proper botanical and cultivar names—it's usual to list herbs by their common names, but each herb seems to have so many common names, both current and historical, that the only way to know *exactly* which plant is being talked about is the use of its correct Latin binomial and cultivar name. To be fair to the merchants, a catalog is really an offer to *sell*: a serious company will tell you all about how they conduct business, and give you the name of a real human being to contact in case of problems. Are all these musts satisfied? Now you can start to compare plant size, shipping distance, season and method, and finally, price. When you find a good source of robust plants, stick with them and tell all your friends about them—they deserve all the business they can get.

One of my favorites is the herb catalog of Companion Plants of Athens, OH; descriptions of both the plants and their uses are extensive and interesting. If I had read up on borage, I'd have found that "The whole plant is covered with fine hairs. . .the flowers and young leaves are delicious in drinks and salads. . .has a cucumber flavor. . .a good source of vitamins and minerals, particularly potassium and calcium. . .and *reseeds nicely.*" The nice reseeding in Ohio is frankly just plain wanton in California! Another favorite is from Nichols Garden Nursery in Albany, OR; they are a little less expansive in descriptions and sell more than just herbs, but they also tell me something of what herbs are used for and all I need to know about how to grow them. They tell me that the first person to set the volatile oil of the gas plant alight was Linnaeus' daughter—how do you suppose it ever occurred to her to try it? Almost the best seed catalog ever published is that of J.L. Hudson, Seedsman of Redwood City, CA: it is literally an education on the whole plant kingdom, including herbs from every continent. He tells us that *Genista tinctoria* in addition to being called broom is also 'woadwaxen' or 'dyer's greenweed', making both an excellent yellow and green dye; the buds were used as substitutes for capers, and its medicinal uses go back to Pliny.

The catalog of Wrenwood of Berkeley Springs in West Virginia has good cultural information on the ornamental uses of herbs as garden plants, full of growing advice and herb lore, as does the catalog from Dabney Herbs in Louisville, KY, Sunnybrook Farms in Chesterland, OH, Taylor's Herb Gardens in Vista, CA and Richter's in Goodwood, ON, Canada, are from long-established companies; their information is concise and professionally presented. On the other hand, the catalog from Bee Rock Herb Farm in Flintstone, GA is only a few photocopied pages, with very brief descriptions, but offering a number of unusual plants. The catalog of the Sandy Mush Herb Nursery in Leicester, NC is both interesting and written in an italic hand so beautiful that reading it is a dreamy trip back in time.

I have mentioned only a very few, but there are many excellent herb nursery catalogs—some with selections so huge that there is only room to list the varieties and give just the briefest plant descriptions. Other catalogs overflow with tussie-mussies, wreaths, teas, herbal pillows and the makings of potpourri, sachets and various herb crafts, listing only a few plants and seeds; the uses and lore of medicinal and culinary herbs fill others; many more deserve mention than there is room for here. When you dash home to your favorite chair, kick off your shoes and toss aside real letters for the new catalogs, you'll have to admit that catalog study is an addiction for which there is no cure. Curl up with a few good ones tonight; it could be the start of your real horticultural education!

To find catalogs from herb nurseries, check the ads in herb and general gardening magazines. Other sources are *The Herb Gardener's Resource Guide* by Paula Oliver; the second edition lists over 500 sources of herbal goods of all kinds (write to Northwind Farm, Rt. 2,

Photo by Elvin McDonald

Box 246-PG, Shevlin, MN 56676), and my *Gardening by Mail 3: a Source Book,* published by Houghton Mifflin, which lists over 1,000 nurseries and seed companies, including many specializing in herbs. ❦

A collection of catalogs is entertaining, educational and seductive. Good plant descriptions with size, plant habit, season and color of bloom are essential.